New Directions for Community Colleges

Arthur M. Cohen
EDITOR-IN-CHIEF

Florence B. Brawer
ASSOCIATE EDITOR

Carrie B. Kisker
Pam Schuetz
MANAGING EDITORS

Serving Minority Populations

Berta Vigil Laden

EDITOR

Number 127 • Fall 2004
Jossey-Bass
San Francisco

SERVING MINORITY POPULATIONS
Berta Vigil Laden (ed.)
New Directions for Community Colleges, no. 127

Arthur M. Cohen, Editor-in-Chief
Florence B. Brawer, Associate Editor

NEW DIRECTIONS FOR COMMUNITY COLLEGES (ISSN 0194-3081, electronic ISSN 1536-0733) is part of The Jossey-Bass Higher and Adult Education Series and is published quarterly by Wiley Subscription Services, Inc., A Wiley Company, at Jossey-Bass, 989 Market Street, San Francisco, California 94103-1741. Periodicals Postage Paid at San Francisco, California, and at additional mailing offices. POSTMASTER: Send address changes to New Directions for Community Colleges, Jossey-Bass, 989 Market Street, San Francisco, California 94103-1741.

SUBSCRIPTIONS cost $80.00 for individuals and $170.00 for institutions, agencies, and libraries. Prices subject to change. See order form in back of book.

EDITORIAL CORRESPONDENCE should be sent to the Editor-in-Chief, Arthur M. Cohen, at the Graduate School of Education and Information Studies, University of California, Box 951521, Los Angeles, California 90095-1521. All manuscripts receive anonymous reviews by external referees.

New Directions for Community Colleges is indexed in Current Index to Journals in Education (ERIC).

Microfilm copies of issues and articles are available in 16mm and 35mm, as well as microfiche in 105mm, through University Microfilms Inc., 300 North Zeeb Road, Ann Arbor, Michigan 48106-1346.

CONTENTS

EDITOR'S NOTES

At the beginning of the twenty-first century, community colleges continue to exemplify historical American core values of providing educational access and opportunity to all citizens and residents. These open-access institutions currently enroll over a third of all students and approximately half of all minority students enrolled in higher education. Thus community colleges serve as the vital gateway to higher education for a vast number of people, particularly students of color.

Recent data from the National Center for Education Statistics (U.S. Department of Education, 2001) show that 39 percent of all African American, 54 percent of all Hispanic, 47 percent of all American Indian and Alaska Native, and 38 percent of all Asian American and Pacific Islander students attend a community college. The rapid enrollment growth of these diverse groups, especially over the past decade, has brought their numbers near majority status on an increasing number of community college campuses. Thus the term *minority* is being replaced with the more descriptive terms *racially diverse* and *emerging majority* to convey more fully these students' presence in institutions of higher education. The sheer number of these students also redefines the notion that they are "nontraditional" college-going students: in reality they are increasingly "traditional" (in the modal sense) and are enrolled in the majority of U.S. community colleges, from Hawaii and Alaska in the West, across the Midwest, and all along the East Coast.

Emerging majority students are creating a cultural transformation that is being felt in nearly every two-year institution. Their dominant presence is forcing faculty and administrators to rethink their traditional modes of teaching and learning and and explore new ways of ensuring that institutional access, academic success, and equal opportunity for social and career mobility are available and culturally appropriate for these groups. In light of these factors, it is critical to examine how community colleges are serving the growing proportion of racially and ethnically diverse students on their campuses.

This volume focuses on how community colleges recognize and respond to the academic, co-curricular, and cultural needs of their emerging majority student populations. Embedded in each chapter is examination of the evolving role these institutions play in community development. This volume addresses, among others, the following questions:

What are community colleges doing to increase the access and academic success of racially diverse students?

How are college curricula, pedagogy, student services, extracurricular activities, and community outreach changing to meet the needs of an increasingly diverse student population?

What can mainstream community colleges learn from Minority-Serving Institutions (MSIs), such as Tribal Colleges, Historically Black Colleges and Universities, and Hispanic-Serving Institutions, that can assist them in responding effectively to the needs of their minority student populations?

The primary audience for this volume consists of community college faculty and administrators, as well as government officials and policymakers who are concerned about the academic achievement and degree completion rates of African Americans, Hispanics, American Indian and Alaska Natives, Asian Americans and Pacific Islanders, and students from other racial and ethnic groups entering higher education through the open doors of community colleges. Community businesses and human resource services may also find this volume of interest.

To set the stage for this volume, the first chapter by Berta Vigil Laden uses Census 2000 data to describe the demographic shifts occurring across the United States and in two-year college campuses and classrooms. The chapter discusses two exemplary campuses to illustrate how community colleges are addressing the needs of their emerging majority students.

Next, Linda Serra Hagedorn looks at how urban community colleges in the nine-campus district of Los Angeles are responding to challenges in educating their highly diverse student populations. Data for these examples are drawn from a longitudinal mixed-methods study now in its fourth year of operation.

In Chapter Three, Margarita Benítez and Jessie DeAro offer an important federal overview of Minority-Serving Institutions under Title III and Title V of the reauthorized Higher Education Act. These include Historically Black Colleges and Universities, Tribal Colleges and Universities, Hispanic-Serving Institutions, and the newer Alaska Native–Serving Institutions and Native Hawaiian–Serving Institutions. The authors then focus on Hispanic-Serving Institutions and discuss several examples of collaborations with universities and businesses that facilitate Latino student success.

Frankie Santos Laanan and Soko S. Starobin examine the educational and socioeconomic conditions of Asian American and Pacific Islander students in Chapter Four. They describe this heterogeneous population, which has a diverse range of educational needs, in an effort to deconstruct the Asian "model minority" myth, and discuss the merits of creating Asian American and Pacific Islander–Serving Institutions (AAPISIs) as presented in legislative bill H.R. 333 now under review in Congress. The authors offer examples of how they identify AAPISIs and discuss these institutions' common student and institutional characteristics. This chapter provides a lens for thinking about who goes to community college, where they attend, and the nature of their specific academic needs.

The next three chapters offer various national perspectives. In Chapter Five, Edwin Meléndez, Luis Falcón, and Alexandra de Montrichard discuss federal policy shifts following the 1996 enactment of Temporary Assistance for Needy Families (TANF), which restructured the welfare-to-work grants and put tremendous pressures on community colleges to form a number of short-term technical-vocational programs in order to train the TANF recipients. The authors report on survey data and interviews conducted in community colleges that represent predominantly emerging majority student populations and serve large numbers of welfare recipients. Their findings are beneficial for policy and educational decision makers who may be searching for new ways to serve this special group of students.

Administrators and faculty leaders struggle daily to find ways to stretch limited resources in order to adequately address student needs. One salient issue for community colleges is recruiting faculty and administrators of color—individuals who look like minority students and can serve as role models and mentors in and outside the classrooms. In Chapter Six, Jerlando F. L. Jackson and L. Allen Phelps use national data to examine the levels of diversity among administrators and faculty leaders in community colleges to assess whether hiring, retention, and promotion of minority faculty and administrators have been commensurate with enrollment trends for racially diverse students.

Chapter Seven, by Jamie P. Merisotis and Katherine A. Goulian, outlines the purpose and goals of the Alliance for Equity in Higher Education (Alliance), a national partnership that emerged in 1999 following discussions regarding the reauthorization of the Higher Education Act. Under the Alliance umbrella, three major professional associations and consortia represent approximately 1.8 million students—about 11 percent of all students enrolled in MSIs. These include the American Indian Higher Education Consortium, the Hispanic Association of Colleges and Universities, and the National Association for Higher Education. The Alliance's purpose is to address African American, Hispanic, and American Indian interests "with one voice." Merisotis and Goulian share examples of how the Alliance is working to create greater opportunities in higher education for MSIs and to recognize and preserve cultural diversity for emerging majority students in community colleges. The final chapter, by Victor Sáenz, presents additional information and a number of key resources for serving minority populations in community colleges.

This volume is just one of many studies, reports, and other publications that address the needs, challenges, and opportunities presented by racially and ethnically diverse students in today's community colleges. It is our collective hope as contributors to this volume that the data presented and the exemplars shared here will help educators and researchers in thinking about researching and educating the emerging majority student populations on their campuses. Their academic success is truly in our hands.

Berta Vigil Laden
Editor

References

U.S. Department of Education, National Center for Education Statistics. *Digest of Education Statistics, 2001*. Washington, D.C.: U.S. Department of Education, 2001.

BERTA VIGIL LADEN is associate professor of higher education and director of the Community College Leadership program at the Ontario Institute for Studies in Education of the University of Toronto.

1

This chapter presents an overview of the demographic shifts occurring in the United States and discusses the associated rapid increase in the number of community college students from diverse racial backgrounds. Profiles of two community colleges offer examples of timely responses to emerging majority students' academic, economic, and social needs.

Serving Emerging Majority Students

Berta Vigil Laden

The growth factor of students of color is the primary reason why racial diversity must work in higher education. Instead of referring to members of these interest groups as "minorities," they should be considered members of "emerging majority" groups.
— S. Betances (2004, p. 45)

Tremendous growth and transformation in U.S. higher education are occurring as students from diverse racial and ethnic backgrounds enroll in increasing numbers. Between 1990 and 2000, the U.S. population increased by 13 percent while the white population *declined* from 76 to 69 percent of the total population. In the same time period, racial and ethnic minorities increased from one-fourth to nearly a third of the U.S. population (U.S. Census Bureau, 1992, 2001).

The proportion of nonwhites in the general population—including Hispanics, African Americans, Asian Americans and Pacific Islanders, and American Indians and Alaska Natives—is expected to continue rising, from the current 28 percent to 39 percent by 2020, and to approximately 50 percent by 2050 (U.S. Census Bureau, 2001, 2004). Nearly half of the 4.3 million minority students enrolled in degree-granting institutions of higher education in 2000 were enrolled in two-year colleges (U.S. Department of Education, 2002b). These students thus constitute an emerging majority in many of these institutions. The increasing presence of nonwhite students, particularly in specific regions, accentuates the fact that community colleges serve as a vital gateway to higher education for a diverse student population.

Current and projected enrollments suggest that community colleges will continue to be the campuses of choice for the majority of these groups.

As the general population becomes more racially and ethnically diverse, so will college student populations. Betances (2004, p. 44) captures the reality of the cultural and numerical rise of the emerging majority populations in higher education this way:

> For the first time in the history of colleges and universities, educators have to do what no previous generation of their peers had ever done before: educate learners who are members of the dominant society along with those who are not; educate those who view the institutions of the greater society as their friend, along with those who do not; educate those intelligent students who come with a middle-class college-learning framework and whose journey is enhanced by developed competencies. . . . along with those equally intelligent students who do not have those skills; educate those who are blessed with a vast network of supporters who provide resources to help them. . . . along with those who are not blessed with such support; educate those who come from well-to-do backgrounds and those who do not; educate those for whom completing post-secondary, higher educational requirements, and earning degrees form part of their rich family history, along with those for whom it does not; educate those whose cultural heritage/interest/racial group identities are positively affirmed in our racially stratified society, along with those whose are not; and educate those who are white, and those who are not.

This chapter provides an overview of demographic trends from 1990 to 2000 that highlight the dramatic changes occurring in the United States, and then presents a profile of today's community college students. Case studies of two colleges illustrate institutional responses to the challenges and opportunities presented by emerging majority student groups. The chapter concludes with a review of the challenges in serving a racially diverse student body and offers recommendations for how community colleges can promote educational and economic advancement for these students.

Demographics of the General Population

Table 1.1 summarizes demographic shifts in the general population between 1990 and 2000. In 2000, Hispanics represented 12.5 percent of the population; African Americans represented 12.1 percent; Asian Americans, Native Hawaiians, and other Pacific Islanders collectively represented 3.7 percent; and American Indians and Alaska Natives represented 0.7 percent. After a 58 percent growth rate between 1990 and 2000, Hispanics edged out African Americans for the first time to become the largest single nonwhite racial group. Asian American, Native Hawaiian, and other Pacific Islanders increased by 52 percent, becoming the second fastest growing racial group in the United States. Although the overall percentage reported for American

Table 1.1. Population in the United States by Racial and Ethnic Group, 1990 and 2000

Race or Ethnicity	1990 U.S. Population	1990 Percentage	2000 U.S. Population	2000 Percentage	Population Percentage Change 1990–2000
White (Non-Hispanic)	188,128,296	75.6	194,552,774	69.1	−3
Black/African American	29,216,293	11.7	33,947,837	12.1	+16
American Indian and Alaska Native	1,793,773	0.7	2,068,883	0.7	+15
Asian, Native Hawaiian, and Other Pacific Islander	6,968,359	2.8	10,476,678	3.7	+52
Hispanic or Latino	22,354,059	9.0	35,305,818	12.5	+58
Other Race (Non-Hispanic)	249,093	0.1	476,770	0.2	+88
Two or More Races (Non-Hispanic)*	N/A	N/A	4,602,146	1.6	N/A
Total	248,709,873	100.0	281,421,906	100.0	+13

Note:

*Multiracial category was added in Census 2000. Caution should be used when interpreting differences between 1990 and 2000 data.

Sources: U.S. Census Bureau, 1992, 2001.

Indian and Alaska Natives did not reflect a change from 1990 to 2000 due to overall increases in population, this group grew by approximately 15 percent (110,000 people) over the ten-year period. The increase is noteworthy considering that American Indians and Alaska Natives have often been ignored or forgotten in higher education policy discussions in light of their comparatively low participation rates.

The 2000 U.S. Census data highlight several other significant changes in the U.S. population. For instance, the Other Race category, which was created to capture the smaller racial and ethnic groups not specifically identified by the census system, nearly doubled in ten years. The addition of a new category Two or More Races also showed that a small but substantial portion (2.4 percent) of the U.S. population identifies as multiracial. Finally, in 1990 the U.S. Arab population was not listed as a separate group. However, in 2000, over one million people (0.42 percent) identified themselves as of Arab or Middle Eastern ancestry, a 38 percent increase from 1990 (U.S. Census Bureau, 2003).

The expansion of the population by 32.7 million people in the 1990s was the largest numerical increase of any decade in U.S. history. Examining population growth by major racial group across the national landscape demonstrates the dramatic impact that racial diversity has on most states as well as on their economic, social, political, and educational systems. Three out of every four Americans born in the 1990s were nonwhite. Nearly one-third lived in a metropolitan area with five million or more residents, and over half (58 percent) resided in the South and the West. The four most populous states were California (32.4 million), Texas (17.8 million), Florida (15.5 million), and New York (11.7 million) (U.S. Census Bureau, 2001). By the year 2000 three states—California, Hawaii, and New Mexico—as well as the District of Columbia had become "majority minority" states, with more than 50 percent minority populations. Texas followed closely with 48 percent. In stark contrast, only six states—Iowa, Maine, New Hampshire, North Dakota, Vermont, and West Virginia—had less than 10 percent minority populations (U.S. Census Bureau, 2001).

The United States has become a mosaic of many races. A highly diverse, multicultural society lives, works, and studies within the U.S. borders. Moreover, projections indicate that by midcentury "the average U.S. citizen—as defined by Census statistics—will be as likely to trace his or her ancestry to Africa, Asia, the Hispanic world, the Pacific Islands, and the Islamic world—as to trace it to Europe" (Kirwan, 2004, p. xxiii).

Community College Student Demographics

Whether one looks at the demographic data publicized in the media, in educational research, in policy briefs, or if one steps onto any one of the nation's approximately eleven hundred community college campuses, two clear facts stand out. One, community college students represent many distinct racial and ethnic groups. Two, these students are seeking out the community colleges in greater numbers to get an education, earn a certificate or associate degree, enhance their job skills, prepare for transfer, or improve their English or basic literacy skills. Table 1.2 describes changes in numbers of community college students from different racial and ethnic groups between 1990 and 2000. The data vividly show the declining enrollment of white students in contrast to the rising enrollments of every other racial or ethnic group, with Hispanics and Asians showing the greatest increases. In sum, the data underscore the growing presence of students from racially diverse backgrounds in community colleges.

In 2000, students of color represented 34 percent of all students enrolled in public two-year colleges and 38 percent of all students in private two-year colleges. More specifically, in at least half of all two-year institutions, racially diverse students made up between 25 and 90 percent of all students enrolled (U.S. Department of Education, 2002b). These statistics support what community college educators already know firsthand: students from nonwhite backgrounds are a visible presence on most campuses, and they constitute an emerging majority on many of them. In fact, the term *emerging majority* as referred to earlier in this chapter captures the essence of the still growing, highly diverse, culturally distinct student populations, whether in reference to one specific racial or ethnic group or to all groups collectively.

A brief examination of the community college student population reveals other trends and characteristics. Women continue to constitute more than half of all community college students, a finding that is consistent across all racial groups. As well, at least 55 percent of all community college students are at least twenty-four years old. Regardless of age, over 80 percent of the students are employed and, of these, almost 54 percent work full time and over 30 percent work part time. In addition, over a third (34.5 percent) are responsible for dependents; of these, over 16 percent are also single parents. In light of these characteristics, it is not surprising to learn that 64 percent of all students enrolled in community colleges attend part time (U.S. Department of Education, 2002a).

Degree attainment is a typical measure of institutional success and accountability. In 2000, the nation's community colleges conferred over 230,000 associate degrees; nearly three-fourths (71.8 percent) of these were awarded to white students. Despite the growing presence of nonwhite students, only 9.6 percent of associate degrees were awarded to African Americans, 10.1 percent to Hispanics, 5.3 percent to Asian American and Pacific Islanders, and 1.0 percent to American Indians and Alaska Natives. An additional 2.2 percent went to students classified as Other (U.S. Department of Education, 2002b).

Continued low degree completion rates for these racial groups are particularly disturbing, especially when compared to these students' rising numerical or proportionate representation in community colleges. In

Table 1.2. Enrollment by Racial and Ethnic Group in Two-Year Public Colleges, 1990 and 2000

Race or Ethnicity	1990 Enrollment	1990 Percentage	2000 Enrollment	2000 Percentage	Percentage Change 1990–2000
White (Non-Hispanic)	3,779,800	75.2	3,652,200	64.1	−3
Black/African American	481,400	9.6	691,400	12.1	+44
American Indian and Alaska Native	52,400	1.0	70,100	1.2	+34
Asian, Native Hawaiian, and Other Pacific Islander	210,300	5.1	389,200	6.1	+85
Hispanic or Latino	408,900	8.7	809,200	14.2	+98
Other Race (Non-Hispanic) or Foreign	63,600	1.3	85,200	1.5	+34
Two or More Races (Non-Hispanic)*	N/A	N/A	–	–	
Total	5,240,100	100	5,948,400	100	+14

Note:

*Multiracial category was added in Census 2000. NCES categories do not yet reflect this change. Caution should be used when interpreting differences between 1990 and 2000 data.

Sources: U.S. Census Bureau, 1992; U.S. Department of Education, 2002.

discussions about these low completion rates, it is not uncommon for some community college practitioners or researchers to add the explanatory caveat that not all students who enroll in two-year colleges have the goal of earning an associate degree. Although that may indeed be true, the fact remains that despite rising minority participation rates in community colleges, low persistence, completion, and associate degree attainment rates impede emerging majority students' upward mobility and participation in four-year institutions. Furthermore, these rates are not proportional to these students' enrollment rates either in the aggregate or by distinct racial group. Asian American and Pacific Islander students are the exception to this, yet even within this heterogeneous group considerable variation in educational attainment occurs (see Chapter Four).

The enrollment surges of students of color in community colleges across the nation have immediate implications for administrators, faculty, and students. Kirwan (2004) argues that three actions are required if colleges are to become more inclusive of minority students. First, higher education institutions must adopt race-conscious and gender-conscious policies to correct for the effects of historical discrimination. Second, institutions must prepare students for participation as citizens in a democratic society; to enter careers of their choice; and to be able to compete successfully in an increasingly diverse national and global workplace. Finally, colleges and universities must support greater cultural diversity and greater inclusiveness in and out of the classroom that enhance all students' learning "by subjecting everyone's provincialism to multiple perspectives" (Kirwan, 2004, p. xxiii).

Critical Responses in Progress

How are community colleges responding to the demographic shift? A number of institutions are working to identify and remove systemic barriers that marginalize or disadvantage portions of the student body. They are exploring new ways to facilitate institutional access and academic success as well as ensure equal opportunities for social and career mobility for culturally diverse groups. Several examples of these responses are offered later in this chapter.

Minority students bring their unique cultures to the classroom (Rhoads and Valadez, 1996; Tierney, 1992; Laden, 1999a, 1999b). In fact, one might call the cultural heritage students possess and bring with them to the community college a type of cultural capital, to borrow Bourdieu's term, that must be appreciated, celebrated, and inculcated into the academic and social environment in order to welcome racially diverse students into the mainstream of the institution. This, in turn, responds to, nurtures, and sustains minority students' entry "*to* college. . . . and. . . . *through* college" (italics in the original) (Hagedorn and Tierney, 2002, p. 5).

Community colleges exemplify U.S. higher education's historical core values of providing access and opportunity for all residents. As such, they strive to live up to the term *democracy's colleges,* which was prevalent in the 1960s and 1970s (Cohen and Brawer, 2003). Perhaps due to this mission, community college scholars, policy analysts, and state and federal decision makers are starting to more seriously consider how community colleges are serving racially and ethnically diverse students (Rendón, 2003).

At the federal level, the U.S. Department of Education is directing its attention to support higher educational attainment and improve completion rates of minority populations through various efforts, including Title III and Title V of the Higher Education Act, and specific White House Initiatives for each major racial or ethnic group (see Chapter Three). Similarly, national partnerships are working to foster the collective interests of students of color. The Alliance for Equity in Higher Education, for example, seeks to strengthen institutional development and leadership; ensure student access, success, and equal opportunity to higher education; and recognize and preserve cultural diversity (see Chapter Seven). In addition, many community colleges have created partnerships with universities and local businesses in order to more effectively support community needs.

Community College Examples: Serving Emerging Majority Students

How are community colleges learning from and responding to the diverse needs of emerging majority students to ensure they have equal opportunities to persist and succeed academically? The following sections describe how two community colleges are addressing and improving instructional and student services for their emerging majority students.

Community College of Denver: Serving First-Generation College Students. The main campus of the Community College of Denver (CCD) is located in the heart of downtown, in an urban campus shared with the University of Colorado-Denver and Metropolitan State University. At least two-thirds of its student body are low-income, and 65 percent identify as first-generation college attendees. Of CCD's total student population, 17 percent are African American, 33 percent are Hispanic, and 8 percent are categorized as Other, making CCD both a Hispanic-Serving Institution according to Title V of the Higher Education Act guidelines (at least 25 percent full-time-equivalent Hispanic enrollment) and a Minority-Serving Institution (at least 50 percent of students are nonwhite) (Community College of Denver, 2004). The college is also a Vanguard College, and subscribes to the principles of a learning college as advocated by the League for Innovation in the Community College (O'Banion, 1999).

In an effort to reduce dropout rates and to retain first-generation students to graduation, CCD created a program in 1995 titled the Access and Success Project, which was designed to increase college access, retention, and completion rates for first-year, first-generation students. Funded initially by a Title III grant from the U.S. Department of Education, it is now supported by a second five-year grant through Title V. The Access and Success Project is infused into four academic centers of the college (language arts and behavioral sciences; business and technology; educational advancement; and health, math, and science) to create an integrated, cross-disciplinary approach to retention (Mills, 2004). Using a social services model for managing clients, the project incorporates the concept of education case managers. Two CCD case managers each manage approximately three hundred students, assuming responsibilities beyond typical counseling duties. Sensitive to students' cultural issues, the case managers act as student advocates, helping students with academic, financial, and personal problems in order to keep them on track academically. The Access and Success Project also assists students with financial aid forms and deadlines, and uses other students—including some from the universities located on the shared campus—as peer mentors, tutors, and role models for first-generation students.

CCD's Access and Success students are required to take at least one of two courses, team-taught by two instructors, that make up the college's learning communities. These courses focus on orienting and socializing students to college, teaching such skills as time management and goal setting, and showing students how to use the computer, make PowerPoint presentations, and perform research on career interests. Finally, the Access and Success Project has developed a computerized early alert system that keeps track of students' academic progress throughout the term and identifies students who may need tutoring or other assistance.

The overall success rate of the Access and Success Project is outstanding by any measure. Between 2002 and 2003, the graduation rate for students in the program increased by 38 percent. This contributed to an overall increase of 14 percent in degrees and certificates awarded by CCD and to a 45 percent increase in graduation of students of color (Mills, 2004). In recognition of its success with first-year students, CCD received the Institution of Excellence award from the Policy Center on the First Year of College. Directed by John Gardner, the Policy Center's goal is to encourage colleges to redesign their first-year programs to improve student experiences (Mills, 2004). Clearly, CCD has created a holistic and successful program for first-year, first-generation college students and serves as a model for institutions seeking to better address the academic, cultural, and personal needs of a diverse student body.

LaGuardia Community College: Serving Students from Around the World. One of six community colleges and thirteen four-year institutions in the City University of New York (CUNY) system, LaGuardia Community College in Queens opened in 1971 with 500 students. By 2002, its total enrollment had risen to 12,599 students; more significantly, its student body represented 140 countries and spoke 104 different languages, thus serving as a microcosm of the world. By 2003 39 percent of LaGuardia's students are Hispanic, 18 percent are black or African American, 20 percent are Asian

American or Pacific Islander, 17 percent are white, and 6 percent identify as Other (LaGuardia Community College, 2004a).

In light of its Hispanic enrollment, LaGuardia is classified as a Hispanic-Serving Institution. However, given the numbers of all students of color enrolled at LaGuardia, it is clearly serving an emerging majority student body. Like many of the nation's community college students, a high number of LaGuardia students are first-generation college goers, are often underprepared academically, work at least part time, have dependents and other family obligations, and aspire to improve their lives. With two-thirds of LaGuardia's students representing different cultures and languages, English as a Second Language (ESL) and remedial English courses are in high demand. Nearly half the students take remedial English, attend a writing lab, and get weekly tutoring. Although financial constraints make one-on-one tutoring impossible, students willingly cluster around their writing tutors in groups of four or five in special study areas set aside for them (Feemster, 2002).

Helping students plan ahead is part of the educational mission at LaGuardia. For example, all students must take courses in the Cooperative Education program to help them plan their future careers. They attend seminars to help them decide if they want to transfer and pursue a bachelor's degree or if they want to work after earning their associate degree. Furthermore, in order for students to experience the work world and different types of occupations, they must all complete a two-semester internship (Feemster, 2002). A wide variety of employers participate in the college's internship programs, including some run by LaGuardia alumni.

LaGuardia students also have the option of participating in two programs offered in collaboration with Queens College School of Education that lead to a bachelor's degree in teaching. Students may consider either a joint A.A.-B.S. program in liberal arts and childhood education or an A.A-B.A. program in liberal arts and secondary education. These joint programs were created as a response to teacher shortages and the need for more minority teachers in New York City (LaGuardia Community College, 2004b).

In addition to providing these opportunities, LaGuardia has developed a diversified and proactive approach to serving special populations of high school students in its community: the college operates a unique set of four high schools that address a range of different needs for secondary students. For example, Middle College High School serves five hundred students who are considered academically at risk. Using an accelerated teaching approach, students complete secondary and college courses to earn both their high school diploma and an associate degree in five years. The International High School, a multicultural alternative educational environment for five hundred recent immigrants, offers a high school and college curriculum combining substantive study of all subject matter with intensive study and reinforcement of English. Robert Wagner High School offers special arts and technology programs for selected students, and Frank Sinatra High

School for the Performing Arts accepts talented dance, theatre, and music students (Feemster, 2002; LaGuardia Community College, 2004b).

Like most community colleges, LaGuardia has experienced a steady decline in funding from its traditional government sources and—not unlike many other higher education institutions—it has turned to external sources for funding. Grants from the Bill and Melinda Gates Foundation helped fund Middle College High School, and several federal grants from Title V for Developing Hispanic-Serving Institutions helped offset budget cutbacks and allowed for much-needed campus improvements. One of the Title V grants is currently being used to upgrade all the campus computer networks, including the classrooms, in order to create full online access for administrators, faculty, and students. Another Title V grant focuses on partnerships between LaGuardia and four-year institutions to increase transfer and retention for Hispanic and other students. Title V grants are particularly important to LaGuardia's success because they may be used for institution-wide changes that benefit the entire campus or for special projects specific to Hispanics. Benítez and DeAro in Chapter Three offer further information on this topic.

As can be discerned from this overview of its program offerings, LaGuardia Community College is clearly serving its constituents in innovative and challenging ways. Although the college still struggles with the same issues faced by any postsecondary institution with rising student enrollments and declining funds, LaGuardia is responding to these challenges and thus offers lessons to other colleges in similar situations.

Challenges and Strategies for Addressing Change

The success of CCD and LaGuardia Community College in addressing the academic needs of their emerging majority students suggests some strategies that other institutions can use to retain students of color, help them become academically successful, and assist them in achieving their academic and career goals. As is true of any best practices, however, the contextual factors are important. Both of these exemplary colleges were able to tap into federal funds and other foundation grants to fund some of their initiatives. Thus the first challenge for any institution seeking to implement similar initiatives is to find financial sources in or outside the existing budget. Clearly, seeking external funding is a demanding, exhaustive task and one that is also highly competitive. Nevertheless, community colleges have been increasingly forced to seek these alternative funding sources in response to declining government support. Foundations such as the Bill and Melinda Gates Foundation, the Lumina Foundation, and the Pew Center, for example, have become much more interested in community colleges and are providing grants for projects that address retention, transfer, and completion rates for emerging majority and low-income students. Similarly, the U.S. Department of Education, and especially the Title III and Title V offices, accept proposals from community colleges with high enrollments of African American, Hispanic, and American Indian students.

CCD and LaGuardia also tapped into their own human resources, recruiting college personnel and work-study grantees to help make a difference for first-generation and minority students. These colleges created holistic approaches that involved faculty in many disciplines, career and guidance counselors, case managers, and peer mentors and tutors. Their goals were to ensure that minority students received the appropriate guidance, emotional support, encouragement, and financial and academic assistance in a caring, nurturing, nonalienating environment to help them become and remain successful. These two colleges also formed partnerships with universities, nearby high schools, and local employers to create and sustain academic and career programs that addressed a range of different student needs. Finally, CCD's and LaGuardia's programs cut across racial and ethnic lines to create inclusive, multicultural approaches for all students while being cognizant and respectful of the cultural diversity among the students.

Community colleges can recruit, retain, and assist students of color in acquiring basic academic and technical skills, becoming academically successful, and graduating or transferring to a four-year university. On the whole, educational leaders and policymakers are not lacking in ideas or strategies, but many do lack a cohesive approach to understanding and addressing the needs of a racially diverse student body. The challenges before each of these groups are multifold as the CCD and LaGuardia examples demonstrate. However, solutions can be found to the challenges of raising student aspirations, providing academic and career incentives leading to greater student success, and securing additional funding sources. Community colleges can tackle these and other challenges by developing and applying an integrated academic, social, and cultural institutional methodology that creates an environment of success for emerging majority students. The following recommendations drawn from the two community colleges discussed in this chapter may be useful to community college leaders striving to create such an environment.

Welcome and Celebrate Students' Diverse Cultures. Fundamental to success in serving minority populations is *how* community college faculty and administrators accept the challenge to transform their institution into a receptive, nonalienating campus that welcomes and celebrates all students' cultural and racial heritage, regardless of socioeconomic background. Research has shown that when an institution not only accepts and celebrates students' backgrounds but also integrates their unique cultural capital into the institution, students thrive and succeed (Laden, 1999a, 1999b; Rhoads and Valadez, 1996; Tierney, 1992).

Create Holistic Approaches. Community colleges must provide the necessary and appropriate programs, curriculum, and instructional and student services to facilitate and enhance students' abilities to achieve their academic and career goals. In their study of seven institutions, Watson, Terrell,

Wright, and Associates (2002) found that students experienced greater academic success when faculty and student service professionals collaborated to create a holistic approach to best practices, and took into account students' social and psychosocial needs both in and out of class.

Teach Navigational Skills. Assisting emerging majority students in learning how to navigate the system—that is, learning how things are done on campus—is important if they are to succeed. Many community college students are the first in their families to attend college, and they need to learn the complexities of how to get information, survive and succeed academically and socially, and adapt to the new environment. Academic support programs such as summer bridge programs, semester or yearlong orientation courses, writing centers, tutoring centers, and peer mentors are some of the ways to help emerging majority students become integrated into the institution. Hurtado and Kamimura (2003) also note that the individuals students encounter in their day-to-day activities also have an impact on their adjustment and socialization experiences. Providing ways for students to connect culturally or emotionally with others on campus can do much to alleviate feelings of isolation and loneliness, and can also lead to sharing information about the system for their mutual benefit.

Develop an Early Alert System. Retaining students of color and providing appropriate guidance are fundamental to improving minority course completion, graduation, and transfer rates. Astin (1993), Tinto (1993), and others found that students who are engaged in their studies and co-curricular activities are more likely to persist and graduate. A consistent monitoring of progress highlights just how engaged students are in the classroom and in their college experience. An early alert system similar to the one at CCD quickly pinpoints students' academic problems and leads to prompt responses and strategies for dealing with them. An early alert system, combined with tutoring, time management, and study skills, may help address students' academic concerns, stress about expenses, financial difficulties, and problems resulting from family and work obligations.

Increase Proportions of Faculty and Administrators of Color. Emerging majority students need to see faculty and administrators who look like them and who can serve as role models, mentors, and advisers. Quality interactions with students of color can facilitate faculty and administrators' personal understanding of student concerns and issues, and interactions with diverse college personnel can increase students' sense of belonging and retention in the community college (Hurtado and Kamimura, 2003). This strategy, however, challenges community colleges to proactively seek, hire, and retain more faculty and administrators of color. At present, the proportion of emerging majority students is much higher than the proportion of faculty and administrators of color. Jackson and Phelps in Chapter Six examine these proportions more closely.

Seek Student Perspectives. Emerging majority students, like any others, like to feel that they matter and that their voices are heard. Research that looks closely at the experiences of diverse student groups in emerging majority institutions is still needed, and there is much to be learned about the student experience from students themselves. As the number of students of color in higher education continues to rise, it will become even more necessary to integrate these voices into inclusive, multicultural experiences, both in and outside the classroom environment.

Conclusion

The number of minority students is rapidly increasing in community colleges. How each community college responds to these students and seeks new forms of academic, social, and cultural engagement with them will determine the success of both emerging majority and white students. The two examples in this chapter, as well as those elsewhere in this volume, offer models of hope and encouragement that serving emerging majority populations is the right thing to do educationally, socially, economically, and morally. Preserving the status quo, even unwittingly, would be hazardous not just to emerging majority students but to all students in community colleges and to society itself.

References

Astin, A. W. *What Matters in College.* San Francisco: Jossey-Bass, 1993.

Betances, S. "How to Become an Outstanding Educator of Hispanic and African American First-Generation College Students." In F. W. Hale Jr. (ed.), *What Makes Racial Diversity Work in Higher Education* (pp. 44–59). Sterling, Va.: Stylus, 2004.

Cohen, A. M., and Brawer, F. B. *The American Community College.* (4th ed.) San Francisco: Jossey-Bass, 2003.

Community College of Denver. "About the Community College of Denver." http://www.ccd.rightchoice.org/About_CCD/index/html. Accessed Jan. 3, 2004.

Feemster, R. "The World's Community College." *National Crosstalk,* spring 2002, *10*(2). http://www.highereducation.org/crosstalk/ct0202/news0602.wcc.shtml. Accessed Jan. 3, 2004.

Hagedorn, L. S., and Tierney, W. G. (eds.). *Increasing Access to College.* New York: State University of New York Press, 2002.

Hurtado, S., and Kamimura, M. "Latina/o Retention in Four-Year Institutions." In J. Castellanos and L. Jones (eds.), *The Majority in the Minority: Expanding the Representation of Latina/o Faculty, Administrators and Students in Higher Education* (pp. 139–150). Sterling, Va.: Stylus, 2003.

Kirwan, W. E. "Foreword." In F. W. Hale, Jr. (ed.), *What Makes Racial Diversity Work in Higher Education* (pp. xxi–xxiv). Sterling, VA: Stylus, 2004.

Laden, B. V. "Celebratory Socialization of Culturally Diverse Students in Academic Programs and Support Services." In K. M. Shaw, J. R. Valadez, and R. A. Rhoads (eds.), *Community Colleges as Cultural Texts: Ethnographic Explorations of Organizational Culture* (pp. 173–194). New York: State University of New York Press, 1999a.

Laden, B. V. "Socializing and Mentoring College Students of Color: The Puente Project as an Exemplary Celebratory Socialization Model." *Peabody Journal of Education,* 1999b, *74*(2), 55–74.

LaGuardia Community College. "2003 Institutional Profile." http://www.laguardia.edu/facts/facts03. Accessed Jan. 3, 2004a.

LaGuardia Community College. "Academics and Pre-High School Programs." http://www.laguardia.edu/academics/highschool_precollege.aspx. Accessed June 1, 2004b.

Mills, K. "A Helping Hand." *National Crosstalk,* Winter 2004, *12*(1). http://www.highereducation.org/crosstalk/ct0104/news~helping.shmtl. Accessed Jan. 3, 2004.

O'Banion, T. *A Learning College for the Twenty-First Century.* Washington, D.C.: ACE Oryx, 1999.

Rhoads, R. A., and Valadez, J. R. *Democracy, Multiculturalism, and the Community College.* New York: Garland, 1996.

Tierney, W. G. *Official Encouragement, Institutional Discouragement. Minorities in Academe: The Native American Experience.* Norwood, N.J.: Ablex, 1992.

Tinto, V. *Leaving College: Rethinking the Causes and Cures of Student Attrition.* (2nd ed.) Chicago: University of Chicago Press, 1993.

U.S. Census Bureau. *1990 Census of Population, General Population Characteristics, United States.* 1992. http://www.census.gov/prod/cen1990/cp1/cp-1-1.pdf. Accessed May 30, 2004.

U.S. Census Bureau. *Overview of Race and Hispanic Origin: Census 2000 Brief.* 2001. http://www.census.gov/prod/2001pubs/c2kbr01-1.pdf. Accessed July 9, 2004.

U.S. Census Bureau. *The Arab Population: Census 2000 Brief.* 2003. http://www.census.gov/prod/2003pubs/c2kbr-23.pdf. Accessed July 9, 2004.

U.S. Census Bureau. *U.S. Interim Projections by Age, Sex, Race, and Hispanic Origin.* 2004. http://www.census.gov/ipc/www/usinterimproj. Accessed Mar. 24, 2004.

U.S. Department of Education, National Center for Education Statistics. *Profile of Undergraduates in U.S. Postsecondary Institutions: 1999–2000.* Washington, D.C.: U.S. Department of Education, Office of Educational Research and Improvement, 2002a. (NCES 2002168)

U.S. Department of Education, National Center for Education Statistics. *Digest of Education Statistics, 2002.* Washington, D.C.: U.S. Department of Education, National Center for Education Statistics, 2002b.

Watson, L. W., Terrell, M. C., Wright, D. J., and Associates. *How Minority Students Experience College: Implications for Planning and Policy.* Sterling, Va.: Stylus, 2002.

BERTA VIGIL LADEN *is associate professor of higher education and director of the Community College Leadership program at the Ontario Institute for Studies in Education of the University of Toronto.*

2

This chapter uses data from the Transfer and Retention of Urban Community College Students project to provide evidence of success among racially diverse students in the Los Angeles Community College District. Through interviews with student services personnel, it also describes the specific efforts that may be responsible for this success. In addition, it provides insight into the current and anticipated effects of severe budget cuts on minority student success initiatives.

The Role of Urban Community Colleges in Educating Diverse Populations

Linda Serra Hagedorn

> We must never forget that all Americans have the right to pursue the American Dream; we must never forget that the community college represents the only hope millions of Americans have of achieving that Dream.
>
> —G. B. Vaughan (1989, p. 7)

Vaughan's words ring true for millions of Americans who are community college alumni and who will forever be grateful for the opportunities provided by these institutions. Many community college alumni relate stories of life change and new possibilities thanks to the open-door admission policies, specific student services, and conveniences of a community college. This chapter explores the ways that one district has assisted students who fall outside the group predicted to "make the grade." Concentrating specifically on the support programs that operate as adjuncts to academic programs, this chapter cites specific examples of quality community college programs that have recognized the need to reach out to minority students and offer additional supports or enhanced opportunities. Although all the chapter examples are concentrated in a specific geographical location, the community college district featured may be similar to other large urban districts and thus the chapter provides useful information for other districts and campuses.

This chapter is an outgrowth of the Transfer and Retention of Urban Community College Students (TRUCCS) project. Beginning as a three-year longitudinal project supported through the U.S. Department of

NEW DIRECTIONS FOR COMMUNITY COLLEGES, no. 127, Fall 2004 © Wiley Periodicals, Inc.

Education, TRUCCS has been funded for an additional two years by the Lumina Foundation. In spring 2001, TRUCCS collected questionnaire and transcript data from approximately five thousand students enrolled in one of the nine campuses of the Los Angeles Community College District (LACCD). Every semester thereafter, the project has collected transcripts and has added attitudinal data from two follow-up questionnaires. The TRUCCS project seeks answers to the perplexing question of how to increase student success (TRUCCS, 2003). Although numerous lessons can be learned from the TRUCCS project, perhaps the most significant is that success is elusive, but when it does occur it is due to supportive institutional structures coupled with administrators and faculty who care about students.

This chapter begins with a description of the case study site: the LACCD. It explains general indicators of community college achievement and then describes LACCD's success in serving minority populations as measured by detailed indicators developed as part of the TRUCCS project. The chapter then uses interviews with student services administrators to illustrate efforts that may be responsible for this success, and concludes with current information regarding state budget cuts and their assumed effect on the programs described.

The Los Angeles Community College District

The LACCD is located in a state currently experiencing a population explosion. According to the 2000 Census, California's population of 33.9 million is 114 percent higher than a decade earlier (U.S. Census Bureau, 2000). Although the state is diverse in all measures, the Hispanic population is growing at the fastest rate. The most current estimates are that Latinos make up 32.4 percent of the state's population and are expected to outnumber Caucasians by the year 2020 (U.S. Census Bureau, 2001). In Los Angeles County, however, the proportion of Hispanic inhabitants is 44.6 percent and is predicted to skyrocket.

More than 130,000 students are currently educated in the LACCD, one of the largest community college districts in the world. Each of the nine campuses offers unique programs and services while sharing a common mission: to provide quality education at a reasonable price to students wishing to transfer, adults seeking to upgrade skills, employers seeking to retrain their workers, and community members interested in lifelong learning (Los Angeles Community College District [LACCD], 2003a). From many angles, the district is truly "emerging majority." Enrollment figures for spring 2003 indicated that 80.9 percent of the students were nonwhite, 37.7 percent were non-native English speakers, 49 percent were over the traditional college age, and 75.7 percent attended part time (LACCD, 2003b). Despite recent fee increases, the California community colleges continue to provide the most affordable higher education in the nation.

Indicators of Community College Success

The measures of success (and nonsuccess) of community college students are almost as diverse as the students themselves. Joining a national movement of accountability, the American Association of Community Colleges and the League for Innovation in the Community College have advocated for indicators and focused definitions to gauge the effectiveness of community colleges in assisting student success (Community College Roundtable, 1994; Doucette and Hughes, 1990). In response to these agencies as well as to public outcries for increased accountability, most state-level Departments of Education have established performance-based measures and standards. For example, Florida includes such student outcomes as the percentage of associate in arts (AA) degree graduates who transfer to a state university within two years, earn a 2.5 GPA or above in the state university system, and go directly into full-time employment and earn at least $9 an hour (Florida Department of Education, 2003). Using a similar model, the Illinois Community College Board developed a system of accountability measures for institutional effectiveness (Illinois Community College Board, 2003). In Texas, the state's education code includes a section on performance measures for public community colleges. By law, each district must prepare an annual performance report that includes such data as course completion rates, number and types of degrees awarded, number of successful transfers, and pass rates for licensures (Texas Higher Education Coordinating Board, 2003).

California has been investigating the appropriate use of accountability measures for well over a decade, and in 1988 passed a state assembly bill that formally charged the Community College Board of Governors and chancellor's office with the creation of a system of accountability (California Assembly Bill 1725, 1988). Education Code Section 71020.5 fosters the creation of an accountability system that is data based and focused on the improvement of educational quality. Performance outcomes at the state, district, and campus levels are monitored through a comprehensive management information system that records such outcomes as course completion, grades, and reenrollment. AB 1725 identified five key areas of concern: student access, success, and satisfaction; staff composition; and fiscal condition. In 1998 the State of California and the California community college system created a performance-based funding program titled Partnership for Excellence, with system goals to increase the number of transfers, the number of awarded degrees and certificates, the proportion of successful course completions, the number of successfully completed apprenticeship courses, and the number of students completing coursework at least one level above prior basic skills enrollment (Office of the Chancellor, 1999). To reach the goals of excellence and to generally assist students, the California community college system has implemented and supported a number of special programs. Chapter Eight provides information on selected programs currently available in the state and in the LACCD.

Findings from the TRUCCS Project

Using both questionnaire and transcript data from the TRUCCS databases, this chapter compares students of color and white students in the aggregate, then specifically reports on Hispanic students because they constitute the largest minority group ("emerging majority") in the district and provide a special focus for many of the district's programs. It is important to note that the statistics presented in this chapter employ terms and definitions used within the TRUCCS project. Where necessary, terminology that may not be familiar to all readers is explained.

Demographics. Accurately reflecting the district, the TRUCCS sample is predominantly composed of students of color. Of the 4,967 students who provided ethnic information, only 575 are white/Caucasian (11.6 percent). For the purposes of this chapter, the minority comparison group includes only those students who identified as African American ($n = 698$), Hispanic ($n = 2,400$), or American Indian/Alaska Native ($n = 10$). Asian American, Pacific Islander, and students who classified as Other were excluded from the comparison group. While all students are deemed important and worthy of intense study, Asian American students were not included in this inquiry because unlike African American, Hispanic, or American Indian students, Asian Americans are not underrepresented in higher education (Koretz, 2001). Furthermore, they are much more likely to complete a bachelor's degree than any other ethnic group (U.S. Department of Education, 2004). While the programs and services reported in this chapter were developed to help all students, they were especially designed to assist those students who have historically been underrepresented in higher education.

A simple statistical comparison of the distribution of students of color and white students by gender and age indicated that students of color were significantly more likely to be female (62.4 percent as compared to 54.1 percent) and below age thirty (72.2 percent as compared to 62.3 percent). Among Hispanic students, 60.5 percent were female, and 77.7 percent were below age thirty.

Course-Taking Behaviors. Stopout—the temporary cessation of enrollment—has been shown to be detrimental to such academic outcomes as degree acquisition and transfer (Warburton, Bugarin, and Nuñez, 2001). The TRUCCS project has developed a measure of continuous enrollment called the continuity index, which is defined as the number of semesters a student completes divided by the number of semesters possible (fall and spring semesters only). For example, a student who first enrolled in the LACCD in spring 2001 and subsequently signed up for courses only during fall 2002 and fall 2003 would have a continuity index of 0.5 (three semesters completed divided by six semesters possible), if the index were calculated in fall 2003. Note that the semester count begins with the first semester of enrollment and ends when the student graduates (receives an associate degree or certificate), transfers, or otherwise achieves his or her stated goal.

White students in the TRUCCS sample had an average continuity index of 0.778, and the index for students of color was 0.771—not a statistically significant difference. When restricting the sample to Hispanic students, the continuity index rose to 0.797, still not statistically different from white students.

To provide another reference measurement for the frequency of stopout, TRUCCS uses a simple measurement called the return rate. Return rates are the proportion of students returning within a window of time. Using a three-year window, the return rate was 79 percent for white students, 84.8 percent for students of color, and 85.4 percent for Hispanic students in the TRUCCS sample. As imprecise as this measure may be, it does indicate that a large proportion of students continue to utilize the LACCD despite periods of stopout.

Retention Issues. Transcripts used in the TRUCCS project reveal that students frequently drop courses but do not drop out or stop out. It is not uncommon for a transcript to show that a student has signed up for a full array of courses only to drop all but one. Or a student may drop all courses one semester only to return to take them again the next. This type of behavior stretches the current definitions of retention, and demands that something other than a dichotomous measure be used. Thus, to quantify retention, TRUCCS uses the course completion ratio, a measure of the proportion of courses in which the student enrolled that he or she successfully completed.

Although in theory the measure of course completion appears simple and straightforward, it is dependent on the definition of an enrollment. Using the definition of enrollment as those courses in which students remained past the "add-drop" window, the 73.9 percent completion rate of white students was found to be statistically higher than the 66.1 percent for students of color. The rate for Hispanic students was 66.9 percent. If enrollments are counted from the first day of classes, however, the completion rates drop to 51.4 percent for whites, 45 percent for Hispanics, and 45.7 percent for African Americans. It must be understood, however, that there are many reasons why students initially enroll in a course that they do not then complete. Some students may enter a course and then discover that it is inappropriate, too difficult, too easy, or just not what they expected. Unfortunately, by the time students make this discovery, courses are frequently closed to other students because all seats are taken. When students err by enrolling in the wrong course, they may preclude the enrollment of another student who could have benefited from the course. Further, another study using the TRUCCS database found that students who frequently "course shopped" were less likely to finish their courses and had lower grades (Hagedorn and others, 2003).

Degree Acquisition Rates. In four-year universities, the acquisition of a degree is the culmination of a goal. Although some students may quickly reenroll for a graduate degree, it is rare for an undergraduate to remain at the university earning multiple degrees. At community colleges, however, it is not uncommon for a student to earn a certificate on the way to earning an associate degree. Although the requirements vary by academic major, the associate degree (AA or AS) generally consists of 60 to 64 units of semester course credit. The academic associate (AA) requires at least 18 semester units of study taken in a single discipline or related disciplines, whereas the associate of science (AS) requires at least 36 semester units in the occupational field. The LACCD offers two types of certificates: the occupational certificate, which, depending on major, consists of approximately 48 units in the discipline; and the skills certificate, also known as the certificate of achievement, which requires fewer than 18 units in the discipline.

In the TRUCCS sample of 5,000 students, 1,487 degrees were awarded to 1,069 students. To interpret this statistic it is important to understand the sampling procedures involved in the TRUCCS project. In spring 2001, five thousand students were recruited to the project through a stratified random sampling of classrooms in the district. All students enrolled in the chosen classrooms were included regardless of how long they had been attending the college, if they had previously been enrolled, or if they had any other type of postsecondary experience. Since the analyses reported were performed three years after the initial data collection, all students had the opportunity to be enrolled for a minimum of three years. Most students had been enrolled for much longer. Students in the sample earned 71 AS degrees, 838 AA degrees, 296 skills certificates, and 282 certificates of completion. About 5 percent ($n = 233$) of the students earned more than one degree. Table 2.1 provides a breakdown of the number of people earning degrees as well as the number of awards. Note that the proportion of students earning an award in each category is included. Degree acquisition was not statistically different for white students and students of color.

Transfer Readiness. The final measure of success covered in this chapter is transfer readiness, defined as the completion of course modules as described in California's Intersegmental General Education Transfer Curriculum (IGETC). In short, IGETC lists the courses that a community college student must take and pass in order to be admitted to a state college with junior status (completion of the general education requirements). IGETC consists of seven modules of courses that when completed with a grade of C or better satisfy the lower division education requirements of the public university system.

For the next set of analyses, the data set was restricted to only those students who indicated on the TRUCCS survey that they would probably or definitely transfer (approximately 70 percent of the sample). This restriction reduced the sample to 363 white and 2,086 minority students, including 1,605 Hispanics. Table 2.2 provides the percentage of students in the three groups that have successfully passed each module.

Table 2.1. Number of TRUCCS Students Earning Types of Degrees (Number of Degrees Awarded)

	AA Degree		AS Degree		Skills Certificate		Certificate	
	Students (degrees)	Percentage	Students (degrees)	Percentage	Students (degrees)	Percentage	Students (degrees)	Percentage
White (n = 575)	81 (83)	14.4	6 (7)	1.0	18 (30)	3.1	26 (42)	4.5
Minority (n = 3,108)	526 (546)	16.9	42 (42)	1.4	119 (228)	3.8	148 (183)	4.8
Hispanic (n = 2,400)	402 (416)	16.7	32 (32)	1.3	74 (111)	3.1	103 (128)	4.3
Total (n = 3,683)	607 (629)	16.5	48 (49)	1.3	137 (258)	3.7	174 (225)	4.7

Table 2.2. Percentage of TRUCCS Sample Completing Specific
IGETC Modules

	White	Minority	Hispanic
English Composition (Area 1)	16.4	16.8	16.9
Math Concepts (Area 2)	27.3	24	26.5
Arts and Humanities (Area 3)	27	20.3	22
Social and Behavioral Sciences (Area 4)	47.7	47.1	49
Physical and Biological Sciences (Area 5)	22.6	17.1	19.6
Language Requirement (Area 6)	6.1	5.4	6.7
History and American Ideals (Area 7)	39.4	46.9	49.6

Reasons for Success: Interviews with Student Services Administrators

To better understand how LACCD programs have provided special assistance to students, we interviewed the vice presidents of student services or their designate at nine community colleges using a semistructured approach. Following a snowballing technique, we asked each subject if there was an additional administrator who might shed more light on our inquiry. Each of the sixteen interviews lasted thirty to fifty minutes. Each interview was taped except in three instances; in these cases, detailed notes were taken because the subjects preferred not to be tape-recorded. All interviews were conducted as "a conversation with a purpose" (Kahn and Cannell, 1957, p. 149), and data from the interviews were organized into categories and coded (Miles and Huberman, 1993).

The first set of interviews occurred during the week that California's governor announced the most severe budget cuts in the history of California community colleges. As can be imagined, the administrators were very busy, but they acknowledged the importance of this topic and provided time for responses to our queries. Although budget cuts would clearly require a reduction in the workforce, and perhaps even cut into the ranks of tenured faculty, the administrators we spoke with emphasized that they were mainly concerned with finding ways to continue serving students. Administrators bemoaned the fact that whole programs that heretofore had assisted minority students would likely be cut.

A theme that emerged throughout the interviews was the importance of special programs in assisting underrepresented students. Several of the interviews involved discussion of the Puente Project that operated prior to the budget cuts on three of the campuses, and of Puente's efforts to reach Hispanic students specifically (the majority population in the district):

> Our academic services are designed to teach all students, regardless of ethnic group, but we do have special programs like Puente, for instance. Puente classes bring in cultural identity and help the students to be proud of who they are. In addition, the special Puente classes teach students to communicate well

both orally and in writing in English—something they need to succeed in the American education system [Campus 1].

When community colleges learned that Puente would not be funded in the future, administrators bemoaned the decision:

> Well, the best way we supported Hispanic students was through the Puente program. Of course the Puente program now is suspended due to budget cuts. I am now only a part-time counselor due to the cuts. Puente is an expensive program to run as it requires a 50 percent release-time counselor, and faculty get a one-course release for being in the program [Campus 5].

Other programs for minority students were mentioned as well. The vice president of student services at Campus 6 indicated that the campus was focused on providing learning communities to help all students, but especially students of color, be successful:

> Learning communities are designed for our students. Now we didn't say "Let's design courses for Hispanic students," but since that is who our students are, that is just what we did! We have coupled English with world history, and we especially emphasize Mexico and South America. This gives the students the opportunity to study their culture and to write about it [Campus 6].

Some of the general programs were reconceptualized to be of special import to underrepresented groups. For example, the Program for Accelerated College Education (PACE) is designed for working adults. The vice president of student services at Campus 2 indicated that she tries to hire faculty for PACE who are both bilingual and bicultural. She explained as follows:

> Mind you it is not a requirement, but when the faculty can serve as role models and can share common ground with the students, I feel that is a plus. Bicultural faculty also are more likely to include culturally appropriate content and to be sympathetic with our first-generation students [Campus 2].

Like those on the other campuses, the vice president of planning and research at Campus 3 reported using Title V funds to both purchase and translate publications in Spanish. Campus 3 also takes concerted steps to have Spanish-speaking counselors and staff. The assistant dean related positive outcomes from their Extended Opportunities Programs and Services (EOP&S):

> Our EOP&S operates from Title V funding. It is a godsend and a lifeline for many of our students. You see, while taking classes is fairly inexpensive, the books are very expensive. It is not unusual for a single textbook to cost over $100. Of course many courses require more than one book. EOP&S provides

funds for books. And the program also provides special counseling—something the students need desperately. There are never enough counselors, and so students usually just ask each other for advice [Campus 3].

Such comments on the value of EOP&S were echoed on several of the campuses. At Campus 9, the vice president of student services bemoaned the fact that funding limited enrollment in EOP&S to only eight hundred students. However, she excitedly spoke of field trips, including the most recent one to Sacramento to rally to the state legislature not to cut funding for community colleges.

The dean of student services and special programs at Campus 1 was quick to tell us about the Bridges to the Future program:

> Bridges to the Future has been very helpful in encouraging our African American and Latino students to go into medicine. In addition to the usual academic stuff, the faculty and staff that work in that program keep a record of who is ultimately successful and goes on to medical school. Every year we have several of our graduates come back and talk to the current students. They love it [Campus 1].

Campus 3 representatives cited other programs, some small, that work to ensure minority student success. For example, Campus 3 has a very small Biotech Academy that works to influence students to enter biotechnology, and also provides internships. Although they are not specific programs, the Fire Technology and EMT academies introduce students to influential people in the field. A program called Afternoon College teaches remedial skills to high school students to prepare them for college. A Machinists Academy specifically targets females, and a Robotics Academy encourages students to pursue an electronics or engineering path. In addition to a staffed transfer center, Campus 3 sponsors a Transfer Hut, which is located in the middle of campus and is staffed once a week to answer questions about transfer.

The dean of planning and research at Campus 5 emphasized their practical programs: CalWorks and the job placement assistance program. CalWorks, or California Work Opportunity and Responsibility to Kids, is a state-based welfare reform program that assists those receiving welfare benefits to eventually become self-sufficient. For those students receiving a Temporary Assistance for Needy Families (TANF) cash grant from Los Angeles County, the campuses provide intake interviews, special orientations, and special assistance with program planning (see Chapter Five).

Serving Minority Students Despite Budget Cuts

At the time of this writing, virtually every state in the nation has been hit with deep budget cuts, and one of the most severely affected states is California. In addition to experiencing the direct repercussions, community college students have also been negatively affected by sharp reductions in the California university systems. For example, budgetary reductions forced the University of California system and the California State University system to decrease the number of transfer students they accepted, thereby reducing access to the university for many students of color (University of California, 2003).

All of the 109 California community college campuses are finding ways of dealing with the budget cuts. At the LACCD, the PACE program was eliminated on some campuses and greatly reduced on others. Students are redirected to evening and weekend classes, some of which are offered in eight-week blocks similar to what was offered through PACE. The Freshman/Sophomore Experience program is also on the cutting block. This program utilizes linked courses, a special orientation, tutoring, peer mentoring, field trips, and additional counseling services to create a learning community and to enhance student cohesiveness and success. According to our interview respondents, however, faculty and administrators at one campus are trying to keep this program going—even adding funds from their own pockets.

Currently, no program is exempt from elimination. EOP&S, which has operated at the district for roughly a quarter of a century, is threatened. Even the highly successful Puente Project has been temporarily suspended on several campuses while staff desperately search for ways to reinstate it (Puente, 2004). Many of the CalWorks offices have greatly reduced their number of hours and staff. Interview respondents at the nine LACCD campuses detailed stories of heroic efforts by faculty and administrators to alleviate the financial situation and weather the cuts until better times returned:

> Bad times come in cycles. But many of our faculty are pitching in by holding special tutoring sessions or using their planning time to supervise students as they study. We have good people who go out of their way to bridge the times between up and down cycles [Campus 8].

If Money Were Not a Problem

Our final question in each interview asked what community college administrators would do to assist minority students if money were not a problem. Virtually everyone voted for reinstatement and continuation of current programs with the addition of others, such as a learning community for older returning adults, mentoring programs for first-generation students, and additional support for students with dependents. Several administrators cited the need for more computers and technology. One of the most passionate pleas was from a counselor in one of the special programs:

> Counselors, counselors, and more counselors. . . . And if there was money left over I would ask for more counselors. Our students need assistance and

direction that they don't get now. We need academic counselors, job counselors, and while we are at it, let's add some social workers, a nurse, and even a psychologist. Oh yes, and back it up with a food services facility and an income-based meal program. When we get serious about transforming folks into professionals we will realize the need for professional assistance at many levels [Campus 9].

Another administrator wished for faculty development programs, increased financial aid, and student tutors, especially in mathematics. Several others cited expanding services to weekends and evenings. One program director immediately took a different route in answering the query. She recommended more and different types of student assessment procedures.

Well it isn't really only about money. We need new types of assessments to meet the needs of students, and then compensatory tools to follow up on the assessments. I want to "bag" the useless testing and initiate more accurate testing at the lower end. Testing, tutoring, follow-up.

An assistant dean recommended hiring more underrepresented minority faculty and administrators to act as role models and encourage more faculty interaction with minority students. Similarly, others cited the need for more multilingual faculty and staff.

Although there are many lessons that can be drawn from this mixed-method analyses of the LACCD, the following thoughts are provided to conclude this chapter.

"Minority" is a misused and confounding descriptor. Districts like Los Angeles cannot be compartmentalized solely by race or ethnic identification. All students have special needs and will likely meet with greater success when placed in a supportive structure.

Student success must be measured using multiple and diverse indicators. Urban community college students are complex and difficult to describe. In order to judge the effect of special support programs, multiple indicators of success must be monitored over more than one or two semesters.

Special programs function best when staff plan for financial ups and downs. Good and bad economic times are cyclic and recurring. During the "up" phase, plans should be put in place so that a program can maintain itself during the "down" phase.

Support does not have to be packaged within a special program. For example, food services, the availability of assessment tools, and other nonprogrammatic assistance may encourage student success.

There is no replacement for dedicated staff, faculty, and administrators. Students spend the majority of their time on campus and in classrooms. If success is to be widespread, programs should involve college personnel in and outside the classroom.

This chapter discussed one urban community college district with an emerging majority student population. Although the focus on a single district may seem a limitation, it allowed a deep and thick description of a large urban district that is similar to many others throughout the nation. The lessons of the LACCD can be applied in other community colleges that are simultaneously experiencing population growth and budget cutbacks.

References

California Assembly Bill 1725. 1988. http://www.academicsenate.cc.ca.us/Local Senates/AB1725.htm#11.5. Accessed Feb. 15, 2004.

Community College Roundtable. *Community Colleges: Core Indicators of Effectiveness.* Washington, D.C.: American Association of Community Colleges, 1994. (ED 367 411)

Doucette, D., and Hughes, B. (eds.). *Assessing Institutional Effectiveness in Community Colleges.* Laguna Hills, Calif.: League for Innovation in the Community College, 1990.

Florida Department of Education. *Florida Community College System.* http://www.fldoe.org/cc/Default.asp. Accessed Dec. 1, 2003.

Hagedorn, L. S., and others. *Course-Shopping in the Urban Community Colleges: An Analysis of Student Drop and Add Activities.* Paper presented at the American Educational Research Association, Chicago, Apr. 2003.

Illinois Community College Board. *Accountability.* http://www.iccb.state.il.us/HTML/system/history.html#accountability. Accessed Dec. 1, 2003.

Kahn, R., and Cannell, C. *The Dynamics of Interviewing.* New York: Wiley, 1957.

Koretz, G. "Economic Trends: Education Hasn't Lost Its Luster." *Business Week,* Feb. 5, 2001, *3718.* http://www.businessweek.com/2001/01_06/b3718098.htm.

Los Angeles Community College District. *About Us.* http://www.laccd.edu/about_us. Accessed Dec. 3, 2003a.

Los Angeles Community College District. *Multi-Subject Reports.* http://www.research.laccd.edu/research. Accessed Dec. 3, 2003b.

Miles, M. S., and Huberman, A. M. *Qualitative Data Analysis: A Sourcebook of New Methods.* (2nd ed.) Thousand Oaks, Calif.: Sage, 1993.

Office of the Chancellor, California Community Colleges. *System Performance on Partnership for Excellence Goals.* Sacramento: Office of the Chancellor, California Community Colleges, 1999. (ED 463 002)

Puente. "Thousands March to State Capitol to Save Community College, Outreach Funding." 2004. http://www.puente.net/capitol_march.3.15.04_pg.html. Accessed May 26, 2004.

Texas Higher Education Coordinating Board. *Strategic Plan for Texas Public Community Colleges 1999–2003.* http://www.thecb.state.tx.us/cfbin/ArchFetch.cfm?DocID=0049&Format=HTML. Accessed Dec. 2, 2003.

Transfer and Retention of Urban Community College Students (TRUCCS). http://www.usc.edu/dept/education/truccs. Accessed Dec. 5, 2003.

University of California. *Facts About the University of California. Report of the Office of Strategic Communications. State Budget Update.* 2003. http://www.ucop.edu/news/archives/2003/Budget%20fact%20sheet%209-17-03.pdf. Accessed Nov. 30, 2003.

U.S. Census Bureau. *State and County Quick Facts.* 2000. http://quickfacts.census.gov/qfd/states/06/06037.html. Accessed Dec. 3, 2003.

U.S. Census Bureau. *Census Data Information.* 2001. http://www.census.gov/main/www/cen2000.html. Accessed Nov. 1, 2003.

U.S. Department of Education, National Center for Education Statistics. *The Condition of Education: 2004.* Washington, D.C.: U.S. Government Printing Office, 2004. (NCES 2004–077)

Vaughan, G. B. *Leadership in Transition.* New York: Macmillan, 1989.
Warburton, E. C., Bugarin, R., and Nuñez, A.-M. *Bridging the Gap: Academic Preparation and Postsecondary Success of First-Generation Students.* Washington, D.C.: National Center for Education Statistics, 2001. (NCES 2001–153)

LINDA SERRA HAGEDORN *is associate professor of higher education, associate director of the Center for Higher Education Policy Analysis, and program chair of the Community College Leadership program at the Rossier School of Education at the University of Southern California. She is also the principal investigator of the Transfer and Retention of Urban Community College Students project (TRUCCS).*

3

This chapter highlights the role of Hispanic-Serving Institutions in promoting the academic success of minority students and discusses successful strategies used by several Hispanic-Serving community colleges.

Realizing Student Success at Hispanic-Serving Institutions

Margarita Benítez, Jessie DeAro

Students of color remain significantly underrepresented at all levels of educational attainment, despite numerous efforts by education and government leaders to facilitate student success along educational pathways (U.S. Department of Education, 2002a; U.S. Census Bureau, 2001). Given the increasingly diverse population in the United States, and the national interest in fostering a skilled workforce and an educated and engaged citizenry, all educators must work to support these students; minority student success is no longer a minority issue.

As noted in Chapter One, community colleges are key entrance points to higher education for students from underrepresented groups. Financially disadvantaged students are often drawn to two-year colleges' low cost, geographical proximity, wide range of study options, and general flexibility. Open-door policies and remedial education programs for underprepared high school graduates are typical of community colleges, and these characteristics help enroll and educate racially diverse students. Unfortunately, whereas significant numbers of these students enroll in community colleges, the numbers who graduate are much smaller, especially when seen through the prism of federally set timelines of three years for associate degrees and six years for baccalaureate degrees. This is a matter of ongoing concern, discussion, and research within the higher education community.

The authors gratefully acknowledge the valuable assistance of Alex Chough and Nalini Lamba-Nieves of the U.S. Department of Education in providing information and analysis about HSIs and about the Title V program.

Community colleges are driven by missions to serve their local communities, and adapting services and programs to changing local demographics and workforce needs is key to the survival and success of two-year colleges. Consequently, they are often rich with lessons on how to address the needs and promote the success of low-income and racially diverse students.

Approximately 17 percent of all nonprofit institutions of higher education enroll a disproportionately high number of minority students in comparison to mainstream institutions and are therefore recognized by the federal government as Minority-Serving Institutions (MSIs). MSIs are entitled to receive federal funds set aside for their institutional development (U.S. Department of Education, 2003b). After a brief discussion of MSIs in general, this chapter looks to the largest, most diverse, and fastest-growing sector of MSIs—Hispanic-Serving Institutions (HSIs)—for lessons on enhancing academic success for Hispanics and other students of color. Because some HSI achievements in promoting student success were made possible by funding through Title V of the Higher Education Act, the chapter will also describe this relatively new funding stream. This chapter concludes with a look at the Latino Student Success project, a collaborative effort among six HSIs, and examines the strategies and challenges related to attaining and documenting Latino student success in higher education.

Profiles of Minority-Serving Institutions

The Higher Education Act (HEA) defines six categories of MSIs, as summarized in Table 3.1. Title III and, more recently, Title V of the HEA form the main legislation for MSIs as well as for other institutions of higher education that meet Title III eligibility criteria. Basic eligibility requirements shared by all Title III and Title V institutions include low average educational expenditures per student, high enrollment of financially needy students, not-for-profit status, accreditation, and awarding of associate or higher degrees.

Whereas HSIs, Alaska Native–Serving Institutions (ANSIs), and Native Hawaiian–Serving Institutions (NHSIs) are primarily defined by student enrollment, qualification as Historically Black Colleges and Universities (HBCUs) and Tribal Colleges and Universities (TCUs) is based on an acknowledgment by the federal government of a historical institutional mission to serve African Americans and American Indians, respectively. Most HBCUs have over a hundred years of experience educating African Americans, and serve a primarily African American student body. TCUs are usually about thirty years old and are primarily based on Indian reservations, whence they draw most of their student body. Unlike these types of MSIs, HSIs can come into existence rather quickly, without a mission statement or overt institutional commitment to serve Hispanic students. The following paragraphs discuss each of these types in more detail.

Table 3.1. Minority-Serving Institutions: Numbers and Statutory Definitions

Minority-Serving Institutions	Total Number	Statutory Definition
Hispanic-Serving Institutions	242	At least 25 percent full-time equivalent enrollment of Hispanic students
Historically Black Colleges and Universities	104	Statutorily identified (94 are currently funded by Title III B) (Title III, Sec. 301)
Tribal Colleges and Universities	30	Statutorily identified
Alaska Native Serving Institutions	11	At least 20 percent full-time equivalent enrollment of Alaska Native students (Title III, Sec. 317(b)(2))
Native Hawaiian Serving Institutions	14	At least 10 percent full-time equivalent enrollment of Native Hawaiian students (Title III, Sec. 317(b)(4))
Minority-Serving Institutions (includes some of the above)	492	At least 50 percent full-time equivalent enrollment of aggregate minority students

Sources: U.S. Department of Education, 2003a, 2002b.

Historically Black Colleges and Universities (HBCUs). Only 12.5 percent of the 104 HBCUs are community colleges (13 institutions); 47 percent have graduate programs, and another 13 percent offer professional degrees. However, 39 percent of all HBCUs have open enrollment admissions policies, including all of the Historically Black community colleges. Ten Historically Black community colleges are located in urban locations or near urban centers (76 percent), and three are found in small towns. HBCUs are located in twenty-two states; roughly a third are concentrated in North Carolina, Alabama, and Georgia. Half of all HBCUs are public institutions, and ten of the thirteen Historically Black community colleges are public.

Historically Black community colleges range from very small institutions with seventy-five students to large community colleges enrolling approximately nine thousand students. All together, Historically Black community colleges enroll approximately twenty-eight thousand students (9 percent of total HBCU enrollment); 49 percent are African American, 32 percent are white, 16 percent are Hispanic, and 3 percent are classified as Other. African American enrollment at Historically Black community colleges ranges from 16 to 100 percent and averages 73 percent. In 2002, African American students made up 70 percent of the students who completed their degrees within three years at Historically Black two-year colleges (U.S. Department of Education, 2002b).

Tribal Colleges and Universities (TCUs). Eighty percent of TCUs (twenty-five of thirty-two) are two-year institutions. Only five Tribal Colleges are found in urban locations or near urban centers, whereas the remaining twenty-seven are located in rural areas. TCUs exist in twelve states, and half are located in Montana, North Dakota, and South Dakota. Eight of the two-year Tribal Colleges are private, and all have open admissions policies. Enrollment in two-year Tribal Colleges ranges from forty to two thousand students, and total enrollment in two-year Tribal Colleges is approximately ten thousand students (67 percent of total TCU enrollment); 78 percent are Native American, 19 percent are white, 1 percent are Hispanic, and 2 percent are classified as Other. The Native American enrollment at each of these institutions ranges from 33 to 100 percent and averages 81 percent. Annual institutional expenditures range from $0.5 to $28 million. In 2002, Native American students made up 82 percent of the students who completed their degrees within three years at two-year Tribal Colleges (U.S. Department of Education, 2002b).

Hispanic-Serving Institutions (HSIs). According to the federal government, HSIs are defined as having an enrollment of more than 25 percent Hispanic full-time-equivalent students. Scores of community colleges have become HSIs because of their mission to serve their local area and the growth of the Hispanic population in the United States from fourteen to thirty-five million over the last twenty years (Guzmán, 2001; Laden, 1999, 2004).

There are approximately 242 HSIs located in fourteen states and the Commonwealth of Puerto Rico; 128 of these are community colleges. Although HSIs make up only 7 percent of all nonprofit colleges and universities in the United States, they account for 54 percent of the total Latino student enrollment in higher education. Approximately 800,000 of 1.5 million Latinos currently enrolled in institutions of higher education attend HSIs, and 500,000 of these students are enrolled in Hispanic-Serving community colleges (U.S. Department of Education, 2002a). Excluding the forty-four four-year institutions in the Commonwealth of Puerto Rico, community colleges make up 65 percent of HSIs in the continental United States (U.S. Department of Education, 2002b).

Roughly 80 percent of Hispanic-Serving community colleges are found in urban locations or near urban centers; the rest are located in rural areas and small towns. Sixty percent of all Hispanic-Serving community colleges are in California and Texas, the two states that account for nearly 50 percent of the Hispanic population in the United States. Eighty-seven percent of Hispanic-Serving community colleges are public, and most have open admission policies. Hispanic-Serving community colleges range from very small institutions with fewer than one hundred students to large multicampus systems with more than fifty thousand students. Annual expenditures of Hispanic-Serving community colleges and community college systems range from $1 million to $300 million (U.S. Department of Education, 2002b).

Latino student success has become an issue that transcends Hispanic communities and HSIs. Hispanics are the youngest and fastest-growing group in the United States; they have increased by 58 percent over the last ten years compared to 13 percent for the rest of the U.S. population (Guzmán, 2001).

Hispanics currently constitute 17.5 percent (4.7 million) of the traditional college-age population (between eighteen and twenty-four years of age), yet they make up less than 10 percent (1.5 million) of the total student enrollment in higher education in the United States (U.S. Census Bureau, 2001; U.S. Department of Education, 2002a). At present, Hispanics have the lowest college enrollment rate of eighteen- to twenty-four-year-old high school graduates (35 percent) as well as low high school graduation rates (64 percent) (U.S. Department of Education, 2001, 2002a). In addition, nearly 60 percent of Hispanic students enrolled in higher education are in two-year institutions, compared to only 36 percent of white students and 42 percent of African American students (U.S. Department of Education, 2002a).

Approximately 31 percent of Hispanic students in elementary and secondary schools are Limited English Proficient (LEP) (U.S. Department of Education, 2003a). Consequently, most Hispanic-Serving community colleges have an appreciation for bilingual skills and typically provide support services for students in LEP or ESL programs. Hispanic-Serving community colleges also have flexible course schedules for part-time students who are working or have family responsibilities.

Among MSIs, Hispanic-Serving community colleges serve the most diverse student populations. In addition to 42 percent Hispanic enrollment, 10 percent of students enrolled in Hispanic-Serving community colleges are African American, 9 percent are Asian American, 1 percent are Native American, 30 percent are white, and 8 percent are classified as Other. Therefore, student success at HSIs is not exclusively a Hispanic matter. Presidents and deans at institutions that receive funds set aside for HSIs are quick to point out that these funds serve to strengthen the entire institution and also benefit students who are not Latino (Santiago, Andrade, and Brown, 2004). Indeed, unlike that of mainstream community colleges, the racial distribution of Hispanic-Serving community college completers is similar to the racial distribution of enrollees; at these institutions, students of all races and ethnicities graduate or complete their degree at the same rates (U.S. Department of Education, 2002b).

Given the broad diversity of Hispanic-Serving community colleges—in terms of location, size, student population, and resource base—student success initiatives at these colleges can provide concrete and valuable blueprints for many other institutions. Because many of the initiatives to enhance student success at HSIs have been funded through Title V of the Higher Education Act, the following section provides more detail on this legislation.

Title V of the Higher Education Act

The creation of the Title V program in the 1998 reauthorization of the Higher Education Act provided a new funding stream specifically for HSIs. Although still rather small by federal funding standards, the program has grown swiftly, both in funds and in participants, as shown in Table 3.2. Title

Table 3.2. Title V Funding History of Hispanic-Serving Institutions

Fiscal Year	Appropriation	New Awards	Total Awards	Average Yearly Award (Thousands per Award)
1995	$12 M	37	37	$325
1999	$28 M	39	76	$368
2000	$42.5 M	69	108	$394
2001	$68 M	49	157	$433
2002	$86 M	34	191	$450
2003	$92.4 M	29	220	$420
2004	$93.9 M	42 (expected)	223 (expected)	$421 (expected)

Source: U.S. Department of Education, Title V program Web site (http://www.ed.gov/hsi).

V invests in many different areas of institutional capacity. The most common include student services and curriculum development, as well as infrastructure development, especially in the area of information technology.

Student Services and Curriculum Development. Improving student retention is a priority for most institutions, and many strategies for doing so are crafted around the profile of the "traditional" college student. Traditional college students enroll right after high school, are financially dependent on their parents, attend college full time, live on campus, and have few work or family obligations. Nowadays, only about 40 percent of college students in the United States fit that definition, yet many federal, state, and institutional measures and policies continue to be based on it (Choy, 2002). Student retention strategies based on the traditional student are especially inappropriate at Hispanic-Serving community colleges, as 69 percent of students enrolled in these institutions attend part time (U.S. Department of Education, 2002b). Because these students have obligations other than their education, retention strategies must be tailored to their needs and realities. These strategies include "on-demand" student services, such as mentoring, tutoring, and counseling, which are often supported by technology for the largely commuter student population.

Some HSIs that are showing promising results in improving student retention are deliberately aligning student support services with academic programs in order to provide effective support environments for students who juggle competing obligations of work, school, and family. One program of this type, developed with Title V funds, is the LifeMap approach in use at Valencia Community College (VCC) in Orlando, Florida. LifeMap is an individualized guide to help students determine when and how to take specific steps to complete degree requirements and attain career goals. LifeMap links all the components of the college—its faculty, staff, academic programs, technology, and services—in an effort to support students from admission through graduation and beyond. LifeMap works at three levels: as a student's action plan for utilizing institutional resources at each stage of his or her academic career; as a student's guide, with step-by-step instructions for making progress toward academic goals; and as a master plan for VCC to articulate its various functions and focus them toward student success. One important component of LifeMap is the Student Success course. VCC has found that graduates of this course average completion and reenrollment rates that are 20 percent higher than those of degree-seeking and college prep students not enrolled in the class ("LifeMap," 2003).

Another Title V–funded comprehensive approach to improving student learning outcomes and increasing persistence is the multistrand student retention program at Cañada College in San Mateo, California. Cañada's ambitious project integrates curricular transformation, development and implementation of new teaching and learning strategies, online career assessment, improvement of students' technological and other key skills, and strengthening of the institution's K–16 pipeline.

After researching model programs, Cañada implemented a freshman experience learning communities program that coordinated "gatekeeper" English and math courses with appropriate counseling and studying. The college purchased PLATO and academic.com supplemental instruction software programs, and the faculty created course modules in reading and essay writing to strengthen students' basic skills. Ongoing faculty development in overall curricular transformation and in particular research strategies was also emphasized. Eight faculty members per year were trained to improve their competence, awareness, and commitment to curricular transformation, and a broader range of faculty received training in designing successful research assignments, in the use of Cañada's online library, and in basic principles of Web research. In the second year, the curricular transformation, skills enhancement, and pedagogy strands combined to focus on encouraging student research and writing.

The results of Cañada's project, now in its third year, have been extremely promising, and the college is using second-year outcomes as baseline data for monitoring the project's success. The various strands of Cañada's project work together toward the goal of increasing the number of students who are ready to transfer to a four-year institution. It is important to note that a major change is already evident in the renewed institution-wide focus on student success. Although not immediately quantifiable, this cultural change will perhaps be the key to Cañada's overall achievements. Cañada's experience suggests that ambitious and transformative projects generate synergies that create more profound changes than the sum of their parts alone (Phyllis Lucas-Woods, personal communication, Oct. 2003).

The preceding examples illustrate how a sustained focus on student success will eventually have an impact on many dimensions of the college experience, including curricular reform and development. Miami Dade College (Florida) is an example of how Title V funding can be applied specifically to curriculum development. In response to local needs, Miami Dade College used Title V funding to establish a new Hospitality Management Program (HMP). The program provides career opportunities for students who aspire to work as managers and supervisors in hotels, restaurants, resorts, cruise lines, and health and geriatric facilities in southern Florida. Collegewide support services and strong community links enhance student success. The program includes internships and mentoring opportunities at area hotels and cruise lines, and meetings with resort, hotel, hospital, and trade show managers. As well, students develop their own personalized education program together with academic advisers. Projected enrollment in HMP under Title V has been achieved four times over, and stands currently at 850 students (David Countin, personal communication, Oct. 2003).

Information Technology and Infrastructure Development. Infrastructure development, in particular information technology (IT) development, is another area in which significant Title V funds have been allocated. Technology has emerged as an important and often critical component in the cost-effective expansion of the scope and flexibility of key services. However, in light of the limited resources of most community colleges and MSIs, educators must implement creative solutions to enable the full development and deployment of technological capacity.

One promising solution lies in the establishment of collaborative partnerships among institutions with similar goals and challenges. In 2001, five HSIs (California State University, Los Angeles; California Polytechnic State University, Pomona; California State University, San Bernardino; and two community colleges, Mount San Antonio College and Oxnard College) received Title V funding to pool their IT resources in order to improve access to information systems and devise solutions to such common problems as vulnerabilities in network security, asset protection, and campus awareness; and lack of qualified human resources, policies, and procedures. The goals of the project, now in its third year, address a broad range of academic technology issues, from network capacity to curriculum development in the booming field of IT security. Staff at all five institutions have benefited from each other's skills and talents by working together to perform network assessments, train IT staff, develop student internship programs, devise policies and procedures regarding network and data security, and support curriculum development activities.

The first step for this partnership was to create a multicampus team of information system security liaisons, with two representatives from each institution. Team members receive frequent training in network assessment tools and procedures, which they apply to their institutions in order to promptly correct critical vulnerabilities, protect their assets, and share best practices. Student internship programs in IT security, as well as a series of security awareness events, involve students, faculty, and staff from every participating campus. An information security training laboratory is under development at California State University, Los Angeles, and will begin to offer courses in 2004. As a result of the Title V grant, each campus has deployed intrusion detection systems, increased IT security awareness, and provided faculty, staff, and students with protection as well as with training opportunities ("Improving Access to Information Systems at Hispanic-Serving Institutions," 2003).

Technologies that assist articulation of academic requirements and credits between two- and four-year institutions are very helpful in facilitating and encouraging students to transfer and continue their education. Such technologies enable community college students to quickly determine their transfer status to four-year institutions and to chart progress toward career goals. Mercy College, a private four-year HSI in the New York metropolitan area, has leveraged lessons learned from its original Title V project in order to secure funding from the Ford Foundation to create a regional partnership among two- and four-year colleges. These include the Borough of Manhattan Community College, LaGuardia Community College, Medgar Evers College, Westchester Community College, and Pace University. The immediate project goal is the development of seamless articulation to four-year universities for students enrolling at any of the participating community colleges.

Through this project, Mercy College will purchase an Internet articulation system that will allow students to see, in an instant, how their current coursework matches degree requirements at any participating institution, all of which will have already assessed students' course transferability. Two state university systems, in Maryland and in New Jersey, have already implemented online articulation programs to facilitate transfers among and between the two- and four-year institutions within their respective systems. Mercy College hopes to make a similar system available among public and private institutions in the New York metropolitan area.

This kind of program will become increasingly essential in providing students with clear pathways toward their goals, in helping community college students choose courses that will count toward their two- and four-year degree requirements, and in serving the many college students who attain academic credits in three or more academic institutions. The Title V grant helped Mercy become more able to respond to the needs of an at-risk student population. This new articulation effort is the next step in providing appropriate levels of service to students who require greater advice and support in order to complete their academic degrees (Joanne Passaro, personal communication, Jan. 2004).

Another important use of technology to enhance student development and success is the electronic portfolio, which has the potential to empower students to share responsibility for and actively engage in the teaching and learning process. Portfolios can also be an extremely effective means of assessing institutional learning outcomes and progress toward goals. The electronic portfolio project at LaGuardia Community College of the City University of New York, funded by both Title V and the Fund for the Improvement of Postsecondary Education (FIPSE), is an unusually comprehensive program designed to maximize the development and assessment potential of portfolios. The project uses portfolios to document student learning, assess program outcomes, and evaluate institutional effectiveness.

After extensive research and planning spearheaded by a collegewide team, a yearlong process of development and classroom testing was launched at LaGuardia in 2001–2002, with the active involvement of twenty-two faculty members. A faculty summer institute was followed by a yearlong seminar that combined training, classroom-based research, and discussion sessions. In 2003–2004, ePortfolio was made a central element of the First Year Academies—technology, business, allied health, and liberal arts—where incoming students are introduced to LaGuardia's academic offerings. Students are encouraged to "collect, select, reflect, connect"—that is, to collect electronic examples of their academic and creative work such as papers, presentations, videos, and graphics; to select those pieces that are most indicative of their accomplishments, capacities, and interests; to reflect on the evolution of their body of work; and to connect it to the larger community and to their academic and professional goals.

Portfolio assignments in three different courses allow for "snapshots" of the student's development at various stages of his or her college career. Student development is then assessed by evaluating achievement in two broad categories: program competencies and core competencies. To assess *program competencies,* faculty compare statements of overall goals developed by each academic program with student portfolio assignments from the introductory and advanced portfolio courses. Attainment of LaGuardia's seven core competencies is assessed collegewide; the assessment plan embeds competency development and assessment into all major programs. Like Valencia's LifeMap, LaGuardia's student portfolios make up a comprehensive assessment plan that will ultimately be used to inform institutional planning and assess institutional effectiveness and goal achievement ("ePortfolio: Welcome," 2003).

Federal Title V funding has had a significant impact on the HSIs' ability to address the broad range of academic and support needs of first-generation and at-risk students. Both Title V and the outcomes of grantee institutions merit increased national attention in coming years, given that the higher education market will increasingly consist of first-generation and racially diverse students. These students will enter college with varying levels of academic preparation, and they will carry a range of competing family and work obligations. Public and private colleges, many already facing serious budgetary cutbacks, expect to admit increasing numbers of students who will require greater shares of institutional resources to succeed.

Title V institutions have served as lab schools for comprehensive, coordinated programs and practices that will help other institutions develop effective and efficient solutions for ensuring student success. The Title V grantee community has developed an extensive network of formal and informal partnerships and collaborations across institutions, some of which are highlighted in this chapter. These collaborations have proven to be of significant value in focusing institutional commitment and in enhancing institutional capacity by leveraging the resources and strengths of partner schools. The promise of these partnerships, and their ability to affect educational policy debates, are also evident in the work of the Latino Student Success project, a collaborative effort of six HSIs.

The Latino Student Success Project

In 2002, FIPSE supported a twelve-month demonstration project titled Latino Student Success at Hispanic-Serving Institutions. The project involved six public four-year Title V grantees from states with large Latino populations—California, New York, and Texas. Four of these HSIs have cooperative Title V grants with Hispanic-Serving community colleges that focus on assisting transfer students to enroll in baccalaureate programs (California State University, Dominguez Hills, and El Camino Community College; Lehman College, City University of New York, and Bronx Community College; New York City College of Technology and LaGuardia Community College; University of Texas at El Paso and El Paso Community College). All of the four-year Latino Student Success (LSS) institutions draw a large percentage of their student body from community colleges (over 40 percent), and they all make a deliberate effort to cultivate and strengthen their links to these institutions. LSS presidents agree that building links with community colleges is a matter of enlightened self-interest and necessary to maintain and increase their own enrollments.

The presidents of the six institutions appointed representatives from the offices of institutional research, academic affairs, and student life to examine institutional data, resources, and practices related to Latino student success. They describe this as a holistic approach that cut across traditional institutional divisions and enabled all participants to look at issues from each other's perspectives, to focus on the needs of the whole student, and to document and validate their data from the start. This experience was augmented by the interaction among the six teams, which included site visits and frequent exchanges of information.

The following areas of inquiry were at the center of the Latino Student Success project: What does it mean to be an HSI? How does an institution demonstrate its commitment to serve Hispanics? What is the definition of Latino student success? What are useful, appropriate, and substantive indicators of Latino student success?

Among the best practices identified in the LSS report was to "Partner with 'feeder' high schools, community colleges, and community-based organizations to increase Latino student access and their preparation for transition to a baccalaureate-granting institution" (Santiago, Andrade, and Brown, 2004, p. 3). This reinforces the importance of establishing transparent articulation agreements between community colleges and four-year institutions. The recruitment of community college students also supports the assertion that many community college graduates are sought-after scholars who often outperform students who began their education at four-year institutions.

The LSS final report also makes an important contribution to the debate about measures of student success: "While the six HSIs concurred that one important element of Latino student success is the completion of a baccalaureate degree, other elements of success, such as student engagement in campus activities, continuous enrollment, employment beyond graduation, and enrollment in graduate education should also be considered in defining student success" (Santiago, Andrade, and Brown, 2004, p. 3). The report underscores the importance of diversifying the measures of student success and redefining federal timelines for time to degree in view of the growing segment of nontraditional part-time students that cannot achieve their education goals without sustained federal student aid. It also highlights the value of collecting disaggregated data on student performance to gauge the effectiveness of institutional programs and services on diverse student populations. The next stage of the LSS project is to identify community college practices that enhance Latino student success. Additional funding is being sought to analyze the persistence of Latino students at selected community colleges, to identify and examine student success factors at participating institutions, and to engage community college presidents in a dialogue about achieving student success. A key tenet of the LSS project, borne out by the experience of the institutions discussed in this chapter, is that presidential leadership is indispensable in attaining the pervasive levels of focus and commitment to student success that bring about institutional transformations.

Conclusions

As the first Title V grantees near the end of their five-year institutional strengthening projects, this reflection on the challenges and achievements of Hispanic-Serving community colleges may serve to identify future priorities for federal support and might help to improve the Title V program. At the same time, the important strategies and methodologies for serving diverse student populations described in this chapter may be useful to the broader education community in order to support the seven hundred thousand Latino students, as well as other underrepresented students, that are enrolled in institutions that are not HSIs but that share their commitment to Latino student success.

Community colleges must collect more data on student outcomes that will enable them to present their achievements compellingly and transcend the specifics of their own institutional circumstances. The paucity of student outcomes data and the scarcity of institutional research at a number of community colleges impede the documentation and validation of many promising practices. Concerted and deliberate efforts are needed to address this serious limitation.

In addition, an issue raised by the LSS project—also a serious concern for community colleges—is the need to diversify measures of student success, particularly time to degree. Given federal guidelines in this area, when a student takes more than three years to graduate, he or she cannot be counted as a success in the community college. A reevaluation of this standard need not mean a departure from high standards of academic excellence for racially diverse students, but should recognize the reality that the majority of students enrolled in community colleges are nontraditional, part-time students.

Enhancing the academic success of racially diverse students requires a purposeful and integrated approach that often results in institutional transformation as well as greater support for students. Minority students are often the first in their families to attend college, and often confront a range of obstacles and challenges in their efforts to persist to a degree. In the past, these challenges were characterized as deficits, and the programs designed to remediate them had goals that fell far short of substantive success. Recently, however, educators have begun to realize that minority students' experiences and range of responsibilities represent significant strengths that can be used in the achievement of academic success.

Developing programs and practices that can promote minority student success requires a reconceptualization of the college experience from recruitment through graduation and beyond. Community colleges were among the first institutions of higher education to recognize the necessity of continuously adapting to local needs and changing circumstances. Consequently, a number of them have become models of promoting the success of racially diverse students. In so doing, they have redefined the boundaries of the individual institution and have realized the fundamental importance of partnerships in achieving a significant and sustainable impact on student success. It is now increasingly common for community colleges to have robust student success enrichment programs that begin in the K–12 system and extend into four-year and graduate programs. These efforts are bound to gain momentum, as higher education trends indicate that the college-going population of the next few decades will increasingly consist of older, working, and more diverse students. Efforts to enhance minority student success will transform the landscape of higher education, and many community colleges are in the forefront of those efforts.

References

Choy, S. P. *Access and Persistence: Findings from Ten Years of Longitudinal Research on Students*. Washington, D.C.: American Council on Education, 2002.

"ePortfolio: Welcome." http://www.eportfolio.lagcc.cuny.edu. Accessed Sept. 2003.

Guzmán, B. "The Hispanic Population 2000." Washington, D.C.: U.S. Census Bureau, 2001.

"Improving Access to Information Systems at Hispanic-Serving Institutions." http://www.infosec.csusb.edu/TitleV/grant.html. Accessed Sept. 2003.

Laden, B. V. "Two-Year Hispanic-Serving Colleges." In B. K. Townsend (ed.), *Two-Year Colleges for Women and Minorities* (pp. 151–194). New York: Garland, 1999.

Laden, B. V. "Hispanic-Serving Institutions: What Are They? Where Are They?" *Community College Journal of Research and Practice,* 2004, 28(3), 181–198.

"LifeMap." http://valenciacc.edu/lifemap/more_lifemap.asp. Accessed Sept. 2003.

Santiago, D., Andrade, S. J., and Brown, S. *Latino Student Success at Hispanic-Serving Institutions Project Briefing.* http://www.edexcelencia.org. Accessed Feb. 2004.

U.S. Census Bureau. *Census 2000 Summary File.* Table 1. Washington, D.C.: U.S. Census Bureau, 2001.

U.S. Department of Education, National Center for Educational Statistics. *Dropout Rates in the United States: 2000.* Washington, D.C.: U.S. Department of Education, 2001.

U.S. Department of Education, National Center for Educational Statistics. *Digest of Education Statistics.* Tables 186, 206, and 334. Washington, D.C.: U.S. Department of Education, 2002a.

U.S. Department of Education, National Center for Educational Statistics, Integrated Postsecondary Education Data System (IPEDS). *Enrollment Survey, Completion Survey, Financial Survey, and Institutional Survey.* Washington, D.C.: U.S. Department of Education, 2002b.

U.S. Department of Education, National Center for Education Statistics. *Overview of Public Elementary and Secondary Schools and Districts: School Year 2001–2002.* Washington, D.C.: U.S. Department of Education, 2003a.

U.S. Department of Education, Office of Civil Rights. *2003 U.S. Department of Education Accredited Postsecondary Minority Institutions.* http://www.ed.gov/about/offices/list/ocr/edlite-minorityinst-as-vi.html. Accessed June 10, 2003b.

MARGARITA BENÍTEZ *has worked as a senior federal official in the U.S. Department of Education, and spearheaded the development of the Title V program for Hispanic-Serving Institutions from 1999 to 2002.*

JESSIE DEARO *joined the U.S. Department of Education as a Presidential Management Fellow in 1999 managing the Title V program for Hispanic-Serving Institutions. In 2003 she joined the National Science Foundation as a program director with the HBCU Undergraduate Program.*

Asian American and Pacific Islanders (AAPIs) represent a diverse group of different ethnicities and cultures. This study examines how national data on race and ethnicity are reported and describes the characteristics of AAPIs in light of the "model minority" myth. In addition, this study examines a definition of Asian American and Pacific Islander–Serving Institutions (AAPISIs) contained in legislation currently under consideration by the United States Congress.

Defining Asian American and Pacific Islander–Serving Institutions

Frankie Santos Laanan, Soko S. Starobin

Community colleges are the post-secondary institutions of choice among many students of color (Cohen and Brawer, 2003). Total enrollment of Hispanic, black, Asian American or Pacific Islander (AAPI), or other non-white students in community colleges increased from 25 percent in 1992 to 30 percent in 1997 (Phillippe and Patton, 2000). By 2000, 34.4 percent of students enrolled in U.S. community colleges identified as black (12.1 percent), Hispanic (14.2 percent), Asian American or Pacific Islander (5.1 percent), or another nonwhite race or ethnicity (3 percent) (U.S. Department of Education, 2003). Hispanic-Serving Institutions (HSIs), Historically Black Colleges and Universities (HBCUs), Tribal Colleges and Universities (TCUs), Native Hawaiian–Serving Institutions (NHSIs), Alaska Native–Serving Institutions (ANSI) and the broader-focus Minority-Serving Institutions (MSIs) may be either two- or four-year institutions. These special-focus colleges typically enroll a relatively large proportion of non-white students or women and often employ specialized services, curriculum, or pedagogy to support the academic success of their nontraditional student populations (Townsend, 1999). Detailed characteristics of these special-focus institutions are outlined in Chapter Three. Qualified special-focus institutions may receive additional federal funding to support programs and services that help many disadvantaged students achieve their educational goals.

As the U.S. student population becomes increasingly diverse, a growing body of publications related to specific student populations has emerged, including "Two-Year Women's Colleges" (Wolf-Wendel and Pedigo, 1999),

New Directions for Community Colleges, no. 127, Fall 2004 © Wiley Periodicals, Inc.

49

"Two-Year Historically Black Colleges" (Guyden, 1999), "Tribal Colleges" (Pavel, Inglebret, and VanDenHende, 1999), "Hispanic-Serving Institutions" (Laden, 1999, 2004), and "The Two-Year Church-Affiliated College and Issues of Access" (Hutcheson and Christie, 1999). Curiously, although AAPI students are a fast-growing population, few publications focus directly on this group. However, legislation recently introduced in the U.S. House of Representatives proposes a new designation—Asian American and Pacific Islander–Serving Institutions (AAPISIs)—which would secure federal funding for qualifying institutions to recruit and retain AAPIs in higher education.

This chapter draws data from the 2000 U.S. Census, the Integrated Postsecondary Education Data System (IPEDS), and other sources to assess the way in which national data on race and ethnicity are reported, provide a demographic overview of Asian American and Pacific Islanders, provide empirical evidence of a growing population in U.S. higher education, and raise awareness of associated critical issues in community colleges. Further, this chapter seeks to operationalize a definition of an AAPISI under consideration by the U.S. House of Representatives that would authorize federal grants to institutions of higher education serving AAPI populations.

Reporting on Race and Ethnicity

The Census Bureau's definition of race is social in nature. Specifically, its definition of race does not conform to any biological, anthropological, or genetic criteria. Instead, the Census Bureau defines ethnicity or origin as the heritage, nationality group, lineage, or country of birth of a person or the person's parents or ancestors before their arrival in the United States (U.S. Census Bureau, 2001).

In the 2000 Census, steps were taken to improve data collection describing race and ethnicity. Unlike earlier data collections, Census 2000 offered respondents the opportunity to report *one or more races* when describing themselves and other members of their households. Thus, for the first time, respondents could identify as multiracial, choosing from fifteen separate race response categories and three specific race areas (Barnes and Bennett, 2002). Eleven of the response categories were specific to Asian American and Pacific Islander (AAPI) groups, including Asian Indian, Chinese, Filipino, Japanese, Korean, Vietnamese, Native Hawaiian, Guamanian or Chamorro, Samoan, Other Asian, and Other Pacific Islander. If an individual chose the category Other Asian or Other Pacific Islander, the individual also had an opportunity to name a specific race.

Even though more specific racial and ethnic data are now being collected, the way in which data are reported still challenges researchers to distinguish between and among racial and ethnic groups. For purposes of reporting, the U.S. Census Bureau collapsed detailed race data into five standard categories similar to those used by the Office of Management and Budget (not including the Some Other Race category). These five categories—which include white, black or African American, American Indian and Alaska Native, Asian, and Native Hawaiian and Other Pacific Islander—have been adopted and used by federal agencies such as the U.S. Department of Education when reporting data by racial or ethnic background (Barnes and Bennett, 2002). For individuals of Hispanic or Latino origin, a separate question on the Census 2000 questionnaire was provided so that they could further define their ethnicity by checking one of four boxes: Puerto Rican, Mexican, Cuban, or Other Spanish/Hispanic/Latino. In addition, these respondents could write in the group or country of origin.

An important caveat about Census 2000 is that the race data are not directly comparable with data collected in previous cycles. In addition, the compression of diverse data into five standard categories tends to obscure unique differences among groups. For example, the category now called Asian is an aggregate variable that includes individuals from Cambodia, China, India, Japan, Korea, Malaysia, Pakistan, the Philippine Islands, Thailand, or Vietnam. Because individuals from these groups are likely to differ in terms of cultural backgrounds, language, social class, and many other characteristics, the larger standard category of Asian may mask important differences between groups. This argument can also be made for Native Hawaiian and other Pacific Islanders. Therefore, the way in which racial and ethnic data are collected and reported poses challenges to researchers and consumers because it does not fully distinguish between and among diverse groups.

Portrait of Asian American and Pacific Islanders in the U.S.

AAPIs are a heterogeneous group of almost twelve million members and constitute 4.2 percent of the total population in the United States. AAPIs are citizens of Chinese, Filipino, Asian Indian, Korean, Vietnamese, Japanese, Cambodian, Pakistani, Laotian, Hmong, Thai, Taiwanese, Indonesian, Bangladeshi, Malaysian, Gaumanian, Samoan, and Other Asian or Pacific Islander heritage (U.S. Census Bureau, 2001). In 2002, approximately half (51 percent) of AAPIs lived in the western region of the United States, 19 percent in the South, 19 percent in the Northeast, and approximately 12 percent in the Midwest. Half of Asian American respondents lived in just three states: California, New York, and Hawaii (Reeves and Bennett, 2003; U.S. Census Bureau, 2001).

Compared with Non-Hispanic Whites. AAPIs demonstrate differences from other racial and ethnic subgroups. For example, almost all AAPIs (95 percent) live in metropolitan areas compared to 78 percent of non-Hispanic whites (Reeves and Bennett, 2003). In addition, AAPIs tend to be somewhat younger than whites—26 percent of AAPIs were under the age of eighteen in 2000 compared to 23 percent of whites. Only 7 percent of AAPIs were sixty-five years of age and over compared with 14 percent of whites. In terms of educational attainment, AAPIs (44 percent) were more likely than whites (28 percent) to complete at least a college degree but were also more likely to have less than a ninth-grade education (9 percent versus 4 percent) (U.S. Census Bureau, 2000). In 2002, 6 percent of the 6.5 million AAPIs in the labor force were unemployed compared to 5 percent of the 103 million whites. A higher percentage of AAPIs than whites were concentrated in managerial and professional specialty occupations (Barnes and Bennett, 2002).

Variations Within the AAPI Population. Educational attainment varies by sex within the AAPI population, as men (51 percent) are more likely to hold a bachelor's or higher degree than women (43 percent). AAPI men have higher participation rates (75 percent) in the labor force than AAPI women (59 percent). AAPI women were most often employed in managerial and professional positions (37 percent), followed by technical, sales, and administrative support (34 percent); service (17 percent); operators, fabricators, and laborers (9 percent); precision, production, craft, and repair (3 percent); and framing, forestry, and fishing (0.5 percent). AAPI men tended to hold managerial and professional positions (41 percent), followed by technical, sales, and administrative support (23 percent); operators, fabricators, and laborers (13 percent); service (12 percent); precision, production, craft, and repair (10 percent); and farming, forestry, and fishing (1 percent) (Reeves and Bennett, 2003).

Myth of the Model Minority

Historically, AAPIs have been viewed as the "model minority"—a community in which everyone is educated, economically successful, and somehow not subject to health problems or social or other barriers in society (Chan, 1991; Lai and Arguelles, 2003; Sue, 1973; Takaki, 1989; U.S. Commission on Civil Rights, 1980). The proposed creation of the AAPISI designation challenges the model minority myth, especially with respect to AAPI college access and academic achievement.

Emerging data reported by the White House Initiative on Asian Americans and Pacific Islanders (n.d.) indicates that approximately one-third of AAPIs speak English less than "very well" and that the poverty rate of AAPI families (10 percent) is higher than that of white families (8 percent). Compared to the total U.S. population, AAPIs are less likely to have health insurance, and less than 6 percent of Tongans, Cambodians, Laotians, and Hmongs have completed college. Many AAPI groups face cultural and linguistic barriers to health and social services.

Recently, Nishioka (2003) raised the question again of whether or not AAPIs are in fact the model minority. Using data from Census 2000, Nishioka provided a summary of the socioeconomic status of AAPIs, including population and immigration, family values, homeownership and housing, education, labor, business, income, and poverty. Noting that both Asian Americans and Native Hawaiians and Pacific Islanders (NHPIs) are compressed into the same U.S. Census reporting category, she demonstrated differences between groups in responses to Census questions. For example, the unemployment rate for Asian Americans was 5 percent compared to 11 percent for NHPIs. The median family income for Asian Americans in 2000 was $59,324 compared to $45,915 for NHPI families. The poverty status by age and race in 1999 showed that 13 percent of individuals categorized as Asian Alone (rather than multiracial) earned incomes below poverty level compared to 18 percent of those identifying as NHPI Alone. Nishioka concluded that AAPI communities are not homogeneous with respect to socioeconomic status. In addition, although there are AAPI groups who have been in the United States for many generations, the wave of new immigrants to the United States has brought individuals with vast differences in terms of education, skills, and financial resources. Nishioka thus concluded that the U.S. Census data do not accurately portray the complexity and heterogeneity of AAPIs.

Proposed Definition of Asian American and Pacific Islander–Serving Institutions (AAPISIs)

In January 2003, Congressman Wu of Oregon introduced legislation H.R. 333 to amend the Higher Education Act of 1965, calling for the authorization of grants for institutions serving AAPIs. Section 318(a) of the bill states: "The Secretary shall provide grants and related assistance to Asian American and Pacific Islander–serving institutions to enable such institutions to improve and expand their capacity to serve Asian Americans and Pacific Islanders" (p. 2).

Section 318(b) of the bill articulates definitions of the specific race and ethnic criteria as well as institutional eligibility requirements for AAPISIs. The definition of "Asian American" in this bill is modeled after that used by the Office of Management and Budget: "A person having origins in any of the original peoples of the Far East, Southeast Asia, or the Indian subcontinent including, for example, Cambodia, China, India, Japan, Korea, Malaysia, Pakistan, the Philippine Islands, Thailand, and Vietnam." The definition of "Pacific Islander" is also modeled after that used by the Office of Management and Budget: "A person having origins in any of the original peoples of Hawaii, Guam, Samoa, or other Pacific Islands." According to H.R. 333, an "Asian American and Pacific Islander–serving institution" would meet four criteria:

1. Be a public or private nonprofit institution of higher education, accredited and degree granting
2. Enroll at least 10 percent AAPI students
3. Demonstrate low educational and general expenditures
4. Enroll a student population, a minimum of 50 percent of whom were degree seeking and were eligible to receive need-based assistance under Title IV (for example, Pell grants, work study, or federal Perkins awards)

Data Sources and Methods

This study examined community colleges located in the fifty United States. Those colleges located in the U.S.–Pacific Island Jurisdiction (for example, Federated States of Micronesia, Palau, Marshall Islands, and Guam) were excluded due to their geographic location. In order to select a national sample of community colleges representing the universe of AAPISIs in the United States, this study used data from the 2000–2001 IPEDS database.

A list of AAPISIs was generated from five IPEDS data files. The first file included such information as institutional name, address, chief administrator, and participation in federal student financial aid programs. Other variables included such characteristics as control, level, affiliation, highest level of degree offering, and degree-granting status. The second file offered data describing such institutional characteristics as award levels offered, accreditation status, and student charges. The third file contained fall 2000 enrollment data by race and ethnicity, gender of student, and level of study of student. The fourth file provided financial information for institutions, including education and general expenditures. The fifth file contained information about the percentage of full-time, first-time, degree- or certificate-seeking undergraduate students receiving federal financial aid. Once variables were selected for this analysis, the five files were merged into a single master file organized by the institutional identification number assigned by IPEDS.

The analytic approach used to identify AAPISIs in this study was descriptive in nature and involved several phases. From a list of all U.S. community colleges, institutions that were accredited by regional accreditation agencies and offered the associate as the highest degree were selected. Starting with the more than one thousand institutions that met this criterion, the second step involved filtering the data to include only institutions that had 25 percent or more undergraduate enrollment of AAPI full-time equivalent (FTE) students (which follows the qualification criteria for Hispanic-Serving Institutions [HSIs]). The final step involved compiling a list of institutions with 10 percent or more undergraduate enrollment of AAPI FTE students (which is consistent with H.R. 333). The next section examines how the AAPISI sample would change depending on whether the AAPISI FTE criterion is 10 or 25 percent.

Results

Table 4.1 rank-orders community colleges with at least 25 percent AAPI FTE students. Because a parsimonious definition of the percentage of AAPI students in the IPEDS data file was not provided, we investigated the extent to which this percentage is based on the enrollment of FTE students. For this analysis, the enrollment data file was used to extract all full-time student enrollments and one-third of all part-time student enrollments to compute the overall FTE counts for each institution. These numbers were then compared with the AAPI FTE student count, which was computed by

Table 4.1. Community Colleges with at Least 25 Percent AAPI FTE Students

Institution	City	State	% AAPI	FTE	Rank
Leeward Community College	Pearl City	HI	81	3,511	1
Kapiolani Community College	Honolulu	HI	78	4,131	2
Honolulu Community College	Honolulu	HI	73	2,787	3
Kauai Community College	Lihue	HI	70	633	4
Hawaii Community College	Hilo	HI	66	1,460	5
Windward Community College	Kaneohe	HI	65	912	6
Maui Community College	Kahului	HI	61	1,562	7
Mission College	Santa Clara	CA	53	4,565	8
Ohlone College	Fremont	CA	41	4,870	9
City College of San Francisco	San Francisco	CA	40	17,819	11
Evergreen Valley College	San Jose	CA	40	6,118	12
Skyline College	San Bruno	CA	40	4,335	13
De Anza College	Cupertino	CA	37	13,197	14
College of Alameda	Alameda	CA	35	2,450	15
Pasadena City College	Pasadena	CA	32	11,867	16
San Jose City College	San Jose	CA	32	5,713	17
Golden West College	Huntington Beach	CA	31	7,000	18
Laney College	Oakland	CA	30	5,549	19
Coastline Community College	Fountain Valley	CA	29	2,940	20
Chabot College	Hayward	CA	28	6,852	21
College of San Mateo	San Mateo	CA	28	5,619	22
Irvine Valley College	Irvine	CA	27	4,777	23
San Diego Miramar College	San Diego	CA	25	3,682	24

extracting all full-time AAPI enrollments and one-third of all part-time AAPI enrollments. Because the percentage of AAPI FTE students in our computation was very similar to the percentage included in the IPEDS master file, we decided to use the IPEDS variable to identify the percentage of FTE AAPI students in Table 4.1.

Twenty-three community colleges in the United States have 25 percent or more AAPI FTE enrollment. The top seven, all located in Hawaii, constitute 30 percent of the sample and enroll between 61 percent and 81 percent of all AAPI students. The FTE enrollment for these AAPISIs ranges from a low of 633 students in Kauai Community College to a high of 3,511 students in Leeward Community College. The remaining community colleges in Table 4.1, all of them in California, make up over two-thirds (70 percent) of the total sample. The percentage of AAPI enrollment in the California colleges ranges from 25 percent (San Diego Miramar College) to 53 percent (Mission College).

To examine which community colleges would qualify as AAPISIs under H.R. 333, a sample of first-time, first-year, full-time students was used to identify ten institutions with at least 10 percent AAPI FTE, as shown in Table 4.2. In each of these institutions, 50 percent or more of the student body received federal financial aid. This figure ranges from a low

Table 4.2. First-Time, First-Year, Full-Time AAPI Students Receiving Federal Financial Aid

Institution Name	City	State	% AAPI	FTE	% Receiving Fed Aid	Rank
Contra Costa College	San Pablo	CA	21	3,626	57	1
CUNY Queensborough Community College	New York	NY	20	7,431	54	2
San Diego City College	San Diego	CA	15	10,902	59	3
CUNY La Guardia Community College	Long Island City	NY	15	8,869	54	4
Montgomery College	Rockville	MD	14	11,829	52	5
City Colleges of Chicago–Harry S Truman College	Chicago	IL	12	6,332	91	6
City Colleges of Chicago–Harold Washington College	Chicago	IL	12	4,515	52	7
Los Medanos College	Pittsburg	CA	11	4,244	75	8
Hudson County Community College	Jersey City	NJ	11	3,630	62	9
CUNY Borough of Manhattan Community College	New York	NY	10	11,848	64	10

of 52 percent (Montgomery College in Maryland) to a high of 91 percent (Harry S Truman College in Illinois).

A few limitations should be noted with respect to Table 4.2. This sample included only first-time, first-year, full-time AAPI students enrolled in fall 2000. This filter differs from the proposed definition of H.R. 333 in which a minimum of 50 percent of the degree-seeking population must be receiving need-based assistance under Title IV. In addition, more data and analysis would be needed to assess whether these institutions meet the H.R. 333 criterion of "low educational and general expenditures." These variations limit direct application of the present study.

Implications and Conclusion

This chapter examined the proposed designation of H.R. 333 to highlight AAPI-Serving community colleges in the United States. Understanding the AAPI constituency is critical to developing culturally sensitive support programs, improved academic advising, and enhanced student success. With a growing population of AAPI immigrants enrolling in community colleges, two-year administrators, faculty, student affairs professionals, and other college personnel must think about how best to serve this important group of students. In addition, racial diversity has been touted as a benefit to society and to educational institutions themselves; establishing AAPISIs is an excellent way to begin incorporating the needs and strengths of AAPI students into the policies, procedures, and ultimately the culture of the community college.

Two-year colleges serve a racially diverse population, and provide initial access to U.S. higher education for the majority of students of color (see Chapter One). However, the growing immigrant population in the United States will have an impact on how community colleges provide access and education for a diverse constituency. Although community colleges already play an integral role in educating and training AAPIs for high-wage and high-skilled occupations, they are in a unique position to model effective ways of serving a significantly growing and diverse AAPI population. Given the economic realities and the competitive labor market, community colleges are in the position to develop and train the human and social capital of this growing population.

Although H.R. 333 proposes a definition of AAPISIs, more research needs to be conducted to provide a portrait of the institutions that qualify as AAPISIs. Specifically, analyses that include both two- and four-year institutions will provide a more extensive and accurate picture of AAPISIs in the United States. Also, studies of AAPISIs located in the U.S.–Pacific Island Jurisdiction should be undertaken. These institutions are unique because of their geographical location, but because they enroll such high proportions of AAPIs, they may offer success strategies applicable to colleges within the fifty states.

Data presented in this chapter provide a starting point for understanding a unique special-focus institution. In addition, the legislation pending in Congress has major political and policy implications for the proposed AAPISIs and their students. Like their counterparts—HSIs, HBCUs, TCUs, NHSIs, ANSIs, and MSIs—AAPISIs serve a growing population of disadvantaged students.

References

Barnes, J. S., and Bennett, C. E. *The Asian Population: 2000.* Census 2000 Brief. Washington, D.C.: U.S. Census Bureau, 2002.

Chan, S. *Asian Americans: An Interpretive History.* Boston: Twayne, 1991.

Cohen, A. M., and Brawer, F. B. *The American Community College.* (4th ed.) San Francisco: Jossey-Bass, 2003.

Guyden, J. A. "Two-Year Historically Black Colleges." In B. K. Townsend (ed.), *Two-Year Colleges for Women and Minorities: Enabling Access to the Baccalaureate.* New York: Garland, 1999.

Hutcheson, P. A., and Christie, R. "The Two-Year Church-Affiliated College and Issues of Access." In B. K. Townsend (ed.), *Two-Year Colleges for Women and Minorities: Enabling Access to the Baccalaureate.* New York: Garland, 1999.

Laden, B. V. "Two-Year Hispanic-Serving Institutions." In B. K. Townsend (ed.), *Two-Year Colleges for Women and Minorities: Enabling Access to the Baccalaureate.* New York: Garland, 1999.

Laden, B. V. "Hispanic-Serving Institutions: What Are They? Where Are They?" *Community College Journal of Research and Practice,* 2004, 28(3), 181–198.

Lai, E., and Arguelles, D. (eds.). *The New Face of Asian Pacific America.* San Francisco: AsianWeek Books, 2003.

Nishioka, J. "The Model Minority?" In E. Lai and D. Arguelles (eds.), *The New Face of Asian Pacific America.* San Francisco: AsianWeek Books, 2003.

Pavel, M. D., Inglebret, E., and VanDenHende, M. "Tribal Colleges." In B. K. Townsend (ed.), *Two-Year Colleges for Women and Minorities: Enabling Access to the Baccalaureate.* New York: Garland, 1999.

Phillippe, K. A., and Patton, M. *National Profile of Community Colleges: Trends and Statistics.* (3rd ed.) Washington, D.C.: Community College Press, 2000.

Reeves, T., and Bennett, C. "The Asian and Pacific Islander Population in the United States: March 2002." *Current Population Reports.* Washington, D.C.: U.S. Census Bureau, 2003. http://www.census.gov/prod/2003pubs/p20-540.pdf. Accessed June 1, 2004.

Sue, D. W. "Understanding Asian Americans: The Neglected Minority." *Personnel and Guidance Journal,* 1973, 51, 386–389.

Takaki, R. *Strangers from a Different Shore: A History of Asian Americans.* New York: Penguin Books, 1989.

Townsend, B. K. (ed.). *Two-Year Colleges for Women and Minorities: Enabling Access to the Baccalaureate.* New York: Garland, 1999.

U.S. Census Bureau. "The Asian and Pacific Islander Population in the United States: March 2000 (Update)." PPL-146. 2000. http://www.census.gov/population/www/socdemo/race/ppl-146.html. Accessed June 1, 2004.

U.S. Census Bureau. "Questions and Answers for Census 2000 Data on Race." 2001. http://www.census.gov/Press-Release/www/2001/raceqandas.html. Accessed June 1, 2004.

U.S. Commission on Civil Rights. *Success of Asian Americans: Fact or Fiction?* Washington, D.C.: United States Commission on Civil Rights, 1980. (ED 216 071)

U.S. Department of Education, National Center for Education Statistics. *Digest of*

Education Statistics, 2002. Washington, D.C.: U.S. Department of Education, 2003. http://nces.ed.gov/pubs2003/2003060c.pdf. Accessed May 31, 2004.

The White House Initiative on Asian Americans and Pacific Islanders. "Asian American and Pacific Islander Facts." (n.d.). http://www.aapi.gov/resources/aapifacts.htm. Accessed Feb. 1, 2004.

Wolf-Wendel, L., and Pedigo, S. "Two-Year Women's Colleges: Silenced, Fading, and Almost Forgotten." In B. K. Townsend (ed.), *Two-Year Colleges for Women and Minorities: Enabling Access to the Baccalaureate.* New York: Garland, 1999.

FRANKIE SANTOS LAANAN is assistant professor of higher education in the department of Educational Leadership and Policy Studies at Iowa State University in Ames, Iowa.

SOKO S. STAROBIN is a doctoral candidate in higher education and a research analyst in the office of institutional research and planning at the University of North Texas in Denton, Texas.

5

Many community colleges have pursued aggressive initiatives to serve students on welfare, creating new academic programs or expanding existing ones. This chapter highlights case studies of best practices that illustrate how institutional initiatives targeting welfare students have resulted in an expanded capacity to educate and serve mainstream students.

Lessons from Community College Programs Targeting Welfare Recipients

Edwin Meléndez, Luis M. Falcón, Alexandra de Montrichard

Community colleges have become key institutions delivering employment training services to the population targeted by welfare-to-work grants (Carnavale and Desrochers, 1997; Meléndez and Suárez, 2001). Many community colleges have developed new programs and structures to meet a stringent set of program requirements and to provide support services for welfare recipients (Katsinas, Banachowski, Bliss, and Short, 1999). Most new programs specifically designed to serve welfare recipients have a significant component of continuing education or noncredit courses such as GED preparation and ESL to develop participants' basic skills. These short-term vocational training programs create links between certificate and degree programs and act as mechanisms to close the gap between training and education (Bailey, 1998; Grubb, 1996). Providing the opportunity for academic and career advancement is perhaps the greatest theoretical advantage community colleges have over other employment training institutions, such as community-based job-training organizations and employer-based training.

Community college success in serving low-income and disadvantaged populations has led to proposals that two-year institutions assume a more central role in regional workforce development systems (Carnavale and Desrocher, 1997; Jenkins and Fitzgerald, 1998). In this study, we examine the ways community colleges have transformed their operations in response

This chapter is based on a more comprehensive study by Meléndez and others (2002).

to the challenges inherent in educating a disadvantaged welfare recipient population with multiple academic and social needs. This chapter examines the following questions: To what extent have community colleges adapted for the welfare recipients entering their institutions? Have the changes in policy induced different responses among mainstream versus predominantly minority-serving colleges? How are curriculum, instruction, student services, and educational programs changing to meet the needs of welfare recipients and other disadvantaged students? What are the institutional factors affecting colleges' participation in workforce development programs? Lessons from case studies and best practices in programs targeting welfare recipients presented in this chapter are particularly relevant to mainstream community colleges targeting nontraditional and minority students.

Welfare-to-Work

The Personal Responsibility and Work Opportunity Reconciliation Act of 1996 (PRWORA) has reshaped and redefined the employment training system in the United States, particularly community colleges' involvement in workforce development activities. PRWORA decentralized authority over welfare programs from the federal government to the states and transformed the public welfare system from an income maintenance program to a work-based system in which public welfare recipients are expected to return to work within a relatively short period of time in exchange for time-limited public assistance. Temporary Assistance for Needy Families (TANF), the major federal program under PRWORA, targets welfare participants who are considered the least employable: those without a high school education and those with low reading or math skills, substance abuse problems, or poor work histories. Welfare-to-work grants target those about to reach their time limit on TANF. Given the characteristics of this population, welfare recipients constitute one of the most challenging populations for whom community colleges provide educational opportunities.

Research Design and Approach

Much literature informed the nationwide survey of community colleges and case studies of selected colleges discussed in this chapter. For example, Grubb and Associates (1999), Grubb, Badway, Bell, and Catellano (1999), and Grubb (1999) refer to the critical roles of teaching methods and course design in community colleges. Meléndez and Suárez (2001) examine effective programs serving disadvantaged Hispanics. Stokes (1996) discusses effective programs serving welfare recipients; Ganzglass (1996) offers an early assessment of the challenges community colleges face in redesigning programs and financial systems to take advantage of TANF funding; and Strawn (1998) and Greenberg, Strawn, and Plimpton (1999) offer analyses and reviews of the policies that affect welfare recipients' participation in college programs. Fisher (1999) offers an assessment of adult literacy education in the success of welfare-to-work programs. Finally, Grubb, Badway, Bell, and Catellano (1999) and Golonka and Matus-Grossman (2001) offer comprehensive analyses of the interaction of program design, support services, and policies in community college programs serving welfare recipients.

Drawing on case studies from prior research, we examined four important functions of programs serving disadvantaged populations: case management and support services, instruction and academic support services, overall program design and integration with other academic units, and links to industry and employers (Meléndez and others, 2002). We theorized that serving welfare participants requires significant resources and changes in all these key institutional functions. These functions must take into account participants' social and educational needs and barriers, facilitate program participation, and provide students with the necessary support and connections to employers and entry-level jobs.

We adopted a two-step method for collecting the data for this study, combining quantitative and qualitative approaches. First, from a list of 1,648 two-year institutions, we drew a sample of 251 colleges. Three different community college samples were then drawn from this short list. The first sample included 116 randomly selected colleges, the second sample drew 83 colleges from a list of 184 Hispanic-Serving Institutions (HSIs), and a final sample of 52 institutions was drawn from a list of 69 Historically Black Colleges and Universities (HBCUs).

Our survey queried administrators about their involvement in welfare-to-work and other programs targeting growing industry sectors (called "hot" programs). We asked whether they had a dedicated staff and a strong case management component in programs targeting welfare recipients and whether these programs were articulated to degree programs. We also inquired about the role of employers in the program. The survey data provided a general picture, based on quantitative indicators, of how much relative progress a particular community college had made in responding to local welfare-to-work initiatives. Using information from the survey, we ranked the colleges in terms of their degree of institutional involvement with welfare-to-work initiatives, and categorized community colleges according to whether they (1) had already implemented welfare-to-work programs and were actively developing new ones, (2) had some relatively small welfare-to-work programs or were in the initial stages of program development, or (3) were not actively engaged in adapting existing programs or designing new programs targeting welfare-to-work participants.

Using our analysis of the survey data, we selected five community colleges that were most aggressive in the development of welfare-to-work programs: two from a large urban area (Los Angeles), two from medium-size cities (Denver and Fresno), and one from a relatively small city in New Mexico. These institutions were not representative of all community colleges in the survey sample or nationally. They were, however, fine candidates for in-depth case studies of best practices with respect to involvement with welfare-to-work programs. The following section describes findings from the national survey of community colleges, and the case studies presented in the following section provide an in-depth examination of the patterns identified by the survey data.

Survey Findings

Profiles of the 251 community colleges surveyed for this study are presented in Table 5.1. As expected, Hispanics constitute the majority (45.2 percent) of students in HSIs, African American students constitute the majority (44 percent) in HBCUs, and whites are the majority (69.3 percent) in the general category (representing a random selection of community colleges). The proportion of TANF students in the 116 randomly selected community college campuses is 6.4 percent. That proportion is lower for HBCUs (4.4 percent) and higher for HSIs (10.1 percent).

Contrary to our expectations, survey results show that the majority of students participating in welfare programs are enrolled as full-time students: 61 percent of those in the general sample, 76 percent of those in HSIs, and 48 percent in HBCUs are enrolled full time. However, only 32 to 44 percent of welfare recipients are enrolled in degree programs. The majority of these students are enrolled in nondegree programs regardless of whether they are full-time or part-time students.

Another important finding is that community colleges have a vast program infrastructure targeting disadvantaged students. Programs designed to address low reading and math skills ranked first among those targeting special-needs populations, and GED preparation courses were also common. Colleges also had support services for students who are parents of young children, have poor work histories, or have substance abuse problems (Table 5.1). The survey revealed that the existence of an infrastructure of educational and social support services is integral to colleges' ability to develop programs targeting disadvantaged students.

As shown in Table 5.2, 85 percent of the community colleges in the general sample ($n = 116$) have designed short-term (three- to six-month) vocational programs to train welfare recipients. This figure is even higher for HBCUs (90 percent) and HSIs (96 percent). Almost all community colleges surveyed offer a variety of support services and job readiness programs to welfare students. Counseling is offered in three-fourths of the institutions; half offer case management and day care, and a third offer transportation and substance abuse services. In many ways, community colleges have adopted services typical of community-based social service agencies. In general, student outcomes from these programs, such as job placement and retention rates, are comparable to outcomes for other training providers in the region. Administrators at community colleges estimate that over two-thirds of students complete the programs in which they enroll, and over three-quarters of them find jobs in the areas in which they train.

Table 5.1. Student Characteristics

	General (n = 116)	Hispanic-Serving (n = 83)	Historically Black (n = 52)
Percentage by race and ethnicity			
Non-Hispanic white	69.3	32.9	41.9
African American	11.7	11.4	44.0
Hispanic	8.9	45.2	7.6
Asian American	4.6	5.9	2.5
Other	5.5	4.6	4.0
Percentage of welfare recipients			
in total student body	6.4	10.1	4.4
Recipients attending full-time	61.0	75.5	48.0
Recipients attending part-time	36.3	24.6	43.9
Recipients in degree programs	46.2	43.5	32.1
Percentage of colleges with programs			
for special needs populations			
Low reading or math skills	80.9	93.8	78.4
Lack of high school diploma or GED	70.4	84.0	62.7
Students with young children	60.5	76.3	45.1
Poor work history	50.0	59.2	52.2
Substance abuse problems	29.4	28.8	26.7

Source: Meléndez and others, 2002.

Another interesting finding is that the majority of these short-term training programs offer college preparatory courses to welfare students and most of them are articulated to degree programs. Therefore, academic work is transferable to a long-term educational program. As shown in Table 5.3, the majority of colleges (52.6 percent) reported that these programs are a mix of old and new programs; only a small portion (15.8 percent) of the programs targeting welfare students were in place before the enactment of more restrictive welfare rules in 1996. HBCUs have created fewer new programs but a higher proportion of these colleges are maintaining older programs. In general, the findings suggest that all two-year colleges have taken advantage of policy reform to mainstream welfare students into such programs as business administration, computers, and medical fields. Enrollment in automotive, manufacturing process technology, and welding technology programs was miniscule; these programs were popular among welfare students at less than 2 percent of the institutions. Of those colleges selected for case studies, nursing, office systems, business, computers, and early childhood education programs were the most popular.

Community colleges' participation in welfare-to-work programs makes them important regional labor force intermediaries, because they not only train the unemployed for entry-level jobs but also provide a stepping stone for academic and career advancement. The survey data indicated that employers perceived the advantages of a college education, and felt that it

**Table 5.2. Percentage of Community Colleges Providing Targeted
Services and Programs for Welfare Students**

	General (n = 116)	Hispanic-Serving (n = 83)	Historically Black (n = 52)
Support services			
Case management	45.5	57.5	32.6
Counseling	74.8	71.1	77.3
Child care	48.2	58.7	34.1
Transportation	36.4	40.0	27.9
Substance abuse programs	31.2	30.6	31.7
Job readiness			
Course work to develop soft skills	96.2	100.0	95.0
Preparatory courses	90.4	87.5	90.0
Tutorial programs	81.1	91.1	84.2
Internships with employers	77.4	81.5	77.8
Type of program			
Short-term training programs	84.9	96.4	90.0
Degree programs	71.2	66.1	78.9
Non-degree programs	82.7	96.4	95.2

Source: Meléndez and others, 2002.

improved employees' productivity in the workplace. As shown in Table 5.4. employers were substantially involved in the design, curriculum development, financing, and provision of instructors for programs. For example, close to 90 percent of surveyed community colleges reported that employers provided internships to participants in welfare programs. Job placement services were inherently related to welfare programs and to employers' participation in such programs. Just as colleges reported high levels of employer participation in programs targeting welfare recipients, there was also a high incidence of providing placement services to welfare students. Over 90 percent of the surveyed colleges hired "job developers" and other specialized staff, such as counselors and instructors, and over 84 percent offered specialized programs in job placement.

More than 85 percent of community colleges developed programming specifically for welfare students. Setting up the programs required innovations in academic program design and expansion of support services infrastructure available to economically disadvantaged students. The vast majority of programs targeting welfare students, including those in popular tracks such as medical and business training, articulated to long-term, career-building programs. Clearly many community colleges have provided the academic and social support services needed to promote the mainstreaming of welfare students. In the following section we report on the findings from selected case studies. These cases illustrate how colleges adapted core functions to meet the needs of welfare students.

Table 5.3. Academic Program Development for Welfare Students

	General (n = 116)	Hispanic-Serving (n = 83)	Historically Black (n = 52)
Program development			
New programs	31.6	21.4	18.2
Mix of old and new	52.6	58.9	40.9
Older programs	15.8	19.6	40.9
Total	100.0	100.0	100.0
Business administration			
Office systems	9.3	12.5	10.4
Business	8.4	7.1	5.2
Supervisor, office administration	3.3	–	–
Computers			
Computers and software applications	7.4	8.2	6.5
Computer technology/information	6.5	4.9	6.5
Electronics technology	0.9	–	–
Medical			
Nursing	13.5	4.9	11.7
Medical (general)	7.0	2.7	6.5
Vocational			
Automotive	1.9	–	–
Manufacturing process technology	1.4	–	–
Welding technology	0.9	–	2.6
Social services			
Early childhood	7.0	12.5	9.1
Special services (counseling)	2.3	–	–
Other programs	20.9	34.8	35.1

Source: Meléndez and others, 2002.

Table 5.4. Employer Involvement and Job Placement Services

	Distribution of Respondents (%)		
	General	Hispanic-Serving	Historically Black
Employer involvement in hot programs			
Help in curriculum design	91.3	92.9	88.9
Internships	89.3	91.7	87.0
Classroom equipment or supplies	79.6	71.6	70.7
Financial support	62.2	60.0	55.8
Providing employee-instructors	59.4	60.3	53.3
Job placement services provided to students			
Staff to support graduates' job search	95.7	93.8	90.2
Courses/training in job search techniques	92.2	96.3	90.0
Programs that connect employers to graduates	84.2	89.7	88.0

Source: Meléndez and others, 2002.

Case Studies of Colleges Serving Disadvantaged Populations

We selected 5 of the 251 colleges surveyed to conduct case studies illustrating the institutional changes associated with proactive strategies to accommodate the special needs of students participating in welfare-to-work programs. These community colleges were Los Angeles Community College (California), Los Angeles Trade-Technical College (California), Community College of Denver (Colorado), Fresno Community College (California), and Valencia College (New Mexico).

Case Management and Support Services. Welfare recipients often have multiple barriers that affect their education and employability. These barriers include the lack of quality child care for parents with children, poor access to reliable transportation, involvement in substance abuse and addiction programs, lack of life management skills or significant or recent work experience, and domestic violence issues. Overcoming these barriers requires that community colleges provide counselors and other support services that facilitate program participants' training and transition to the workforce. Through these special programs, counselors give individualized attention to participants and organize group sessions for life management and job readiness.

In addition to having strong case management systems and group activities, some community colleges formally organized students into cohorts and assigned a shared "block" schedule. The effect of this type of program structure is the creation of a smaller and more manageable school environment within the larger community college infrastructure. A "small school" environment is particularly important when students begin the program, and typically includes a range of support services from special programs for women and the disabled to referrals for housing or substance abuse counseling and treatment.

Almost all community colleges included in the study provided day-care facilities or made arrangements with outside providers to serve students. For example, the Valencia campus created a specialized program to respond to the reality that domestic violence is a critical problem for welfare participants. In Fresno, the college adopted a "community job center" strategy modeled after two existing programs, a successful center targeting the needs of immigrant workers and a program serving disabled students. The Denver campus adopted a "track" model whereby the counselor serves as case manager for a small cohort of program participants who have chosen a particular vocational track, such as bank teller training.

The programs and services provided by the case study colleges suggest a set of common strategies that other community colleges may be able to use to reach their nontraditional students. First, create a manageable "small school" environment by forming student cohorts and assigning case managers to work closely with them. Second, leverage the internal and external network of existing resources supporting adult learners in community colleges to support the welfare-to-work initiative. Community colleges have numerous specialized service centers and offices, and partnerships with community-based organizations and local social service agencies can play a pivotal role in sustaining programs serving disadvantaged populations.

Instruction and Academic Support Services. Prior studies (Holzer, 1996; Moss and Tilly, 2001; Salzman, Moss, and Tilly, 1998) have identified a lack of basic skills and workplace socialization as important barriers to employment. Practitioners supervising welfare-to-work programs in community colleges also observe that participants in recent cohorts are in greater need of extensive remedial education and have had fewer workplace experiences than participants in the past. Regardless of whether prospective students have completed high school, most new welfare-to-work students have a functional English literacy of below the ninth-grade level. Typically, effective job training programs for welfare recipients use student-focused instructional practices to support the development of basic skills, including tutorials and competency-based vocational training to provide contextual learning opportunities for students (Gueron and Hamilton, 2002; Strawn, 1998).

The community colleges highlighted in this study set up basic skills learning centers and labs that specialize in remedial education for incoming students. Special programs adapt basic academic skills instruction to vocational contexts either as separate modules or integrated into vocational skill courses. For example, Los Angeles Trade-Technical College (LATTC) used state funding for welfare-to-work programs to create a new Learning Skills Center. The new center consolidated in one location academic improvement programs already in existence; added computer-aided self-paced instruction, lab monitors, and additional instructors; scheduled workshops and discussion sessions on a regular basis; and extended its hours of operation. Similarly, Los Angeles Community College (LACC) operates a learning skills center and offers special sessions for students enrolled in the welfare-to-work program.

In Denver and Valencia, GED preparation was incorporated into the basic program curriculum. Denver's strategy is based on vocational tracks for specific occupations, such as bank teller or health technician, and requires students to have a high school diploma. Valencia, a two-year campus of the University of New Mexico, faced a particularly challenging situation due to the relatively low literacy rates of incoming welfare-to-work students. The college created the Student Enrichment Center to provide one-on-one tutoring and study groups in math and English. The Adult Education Center specializes in GED preparation, basic education, ESL, employability skills, and time management and study skills. Valencia also operates a leadership skills center that included 30 percent welfare-to-work program participants.

Fresno Community College offers comprehensive academic support services through its Vocational Training Center. In operation for more than a decade, this tuition-free center is modeled after best practices in community-based employment training (Meléndez, 1996; Meléndez and Harrison, 1998) and has a job placement rate of 97 percent. The center offers an open entry–open exit format so students can enroll at the start of every week after a brief orientation and proceed through the training modules at their own pace. Training is based on hands-on, contextual learning so students start practicing and modeling the occupation from the beginning of training. In addition to providing job training, the college has thirteen short-term vocational certificates designed for welfare-to-work program participants.

Instructional Practices. Perin (1998) suggests that instructional practices are the hardest area to change, particularly in the context of integrated academic and vocational education. There are some qualitative indicators that suggest welfare-to-work initiatives are improving non-welfare-related instructional practices in community colleges. For example, the Human Services Department at LACC offers two certificates (generalist and drug and alcohol rehabilitation) designed to incorporate pedagogy proven effective with other disadvantaged students. The new LATTC Learning Skills Center is another example of a service that was started to target welfare recipients but now serves all students in the college. However, both changing instruction methods beyond basic education remedial courses and developing new academic support services are relatively slow processes and are more difficult to track and monitor. The evidence from our study suggests that different departments are also beginning to implement pedagogy that better serves welfare-to-work students. In sum, community college responses to the challenge of serving educationally disadvantaged students, both across the institution and within departments, indicate that they have the infrastructure and the experience to continue to develop and establish appropriate and effective programs serving this population.

Program Design and Development. Effective training programs mimic the time rhythms and business culture of the workplace, offer block scheduling, create small learning communities, and are often linked to more advanced training opportunities. For welfare recipients, job placement and postplacement support services are important as well; they help individuals adapt to their new work environment and maintain momentum. Community colleges face a dual challenge, however. First, to qualify for federal training grants, programs must be structured to ensure that students satisfy minimum work hours and other local welfare-to-work program requirements. At the same time, courses must comply with content and length guidelines set forth by educational regulatory agencies such as state education departments and accreditation councils. Program design and development is the area in which state policies and the views of state officials most affect the role that community colleges can play (Meléndez, Falcón, and Bivens, 2003). We next examine two local initiatives to illustrate the influence of policy on program design and development.

California. The most comprehensive program linking welfare-to-work programs to community colleges was in California, which designated $66 million to help institutions assimilate welfare recipients into their programs. State funding allowed department chairs to pay faculty and staff additional compensation to develop new courses and file necessary paperwork. Community colleges were able to hire additional staff and take some risks in their programming. The California community colleges selected for the study were Fresno City College, LATTC, and LACC, whose academic departments began by adapting existing programs to meet welfare-to-work program requirements. The basic restructuring of these courses involved grouping existing introductory vocational courses (for example, office assistant classes) with remedial courses in basic education, life management skills, and job readiness. To accommodate work activity regulations, these courses were offered for more hours during the week, often based on a nine-week schedule (about half a semester). Almost all programs placed students in internships or work-study jobs.

The initial phase of program development was followed by an effort to replicate successful programs and target segments of the job market not previously served by community colleges. In a second round of program design, LACC leadership implemented block scheduling to harmonize and combine new courses with other departmental programs, emphasizing "back-to-back" courses and "back-to-work" in their marketing. Courses were offered in sequence so that students who attended two afternoons and two evenings could get their associate degree in two years. By design, the new programs targeted fast-growing occupations and depended on already existing relationships with industry partners for internships, curriculum design, and adjunct faculty to teach new courses.

Colorado. Colorado's welfare-to-work initiative required the replication of short-term training with new occupational tracks. The tracks have two basic design characteristics: they target particular entry-level positions, such as bank teller or health technician, within an expanding industry, and train candidates specifically for anticipated job openings in the region. At the Community College of Denver, training is organized into three stages combining classroom discussions with a workplace internship. Training focuses on job readiness workshops and a minimum of cooperative work the first month. For three months students spend eighteen hours in basic and vocational education on campus and twenty-two hours at work each week. Students also have a workplace mentor, an experienced worker who can answer work-related questions and help solve everyday problems. During the last stage of the program, students work full time and attend weekly sessions with the track coordinator who monitors their progress for the next three months. The staggered training design of the model appears to work well for introducing inexperienced workers to the rigors of the workplace and has produced high placement and retention rates.

These examples suggest that community colleges are pursuing two somewhat different strategies in taking welfare-to-work programs to scale. The Los Angeles community colleges are "widening" the number of programs that comply with welfare-to-work requirements, and articulating short-term training to certificate and degree programs. They are focused on working within academic departments to create new programs to accommodate an increasing number of students. In Denver, and to some extent in Valencia, the colleges are pursuing a "deepening" strategy that replicates short-term vocational training modules that target new occupations. Fresno follows a blended model: the Vocational Training Center pursues a sectoral strategy very similar to the Community College of Denver, while the academic departments' strategy more closely resembles the Los Angeles colleges. Both strategies have proven successful in different contexts. The key is to apply the correct strategy in the appropriate situation. Sectoral strategies are more associated with dedicated (or stand-alone) programs and short-term training modules. An academic department "deepening" strategy is appropriate for short-term vocational training programs that are more closely related and serve as feeders to established certificate and degree programs. This strategy also involves the redesign and expansion of existing certificate and degree programs.

Links to Industry. Perhaps the most important characteristic of effective training programs is training students in skills relevant to local industry. Effective programs engage employers in the design of the program, course content, and curriculum development, and often include an emphasis in so-called soft skills, such as workers' ability to communicate with coworkers, supervisors, and customers; use problem-solving skills; and adopt an appropriate business attitude. Programs also include cooperative agreements with industry and internships that benefit both students—who are provided with work experience and exposed to workplace demands and expectations—and employers, who get to know prospective workers before they hire them. In this context, job placement is not seen as a separate, last stage of the training but as an integrated part of the training program.

One of the salient characteristics of the colleges included in this study is the maintenance of long-term, well-established relationships with employers and local social and labor agencies. For example, community colleges in California established relations with industry through the different academic departments as part of their regular program operations. As a technical institution with a focus on training for trade industries, LATTC has invited industry leaders to become advisers to the programs and help them design internships, projects, and curricula. Departments also regularly hire adjunct faculty from local industry to teach vocational courses.

The LACC Human Services department requires three internship rotations of about ten hours per week, with each rotation lasting a semester. This regime is part of the socialization to a profession through which students learn many of the core competencies from hands-on experience. In order to provide these experiences for students, community college departments must constantly coordinate activities with industry and foster a vast set of relationships to satisfy demands for internships and placements. Similarly, Fresno Community College has an aggressive policy of work-study internships implemented through different departments. The college's vocational skills training programs involve cooperative work agreements with all the trades and subsidize up to 75 percent of work-study internships.

The Denver strategy is built on the concept of a progressive transition from internships to the workplace. In some cases, employers fully absorb the internship cost. For example, the Northwest Bank's WINGS program absorbs the cost of the internship in compliance with local banking industry regulations, pays intern wages above the federal minimum wage, and promotes almost all participants to full-time employees after four months of training. The program's success is attributed to training interns for the specific teller position that the bank needs to fill at the moment and by providing them with skills specific to the bank's operations. The program then recommends interns for "on-time" interviews for openings in the different branches—that is, when the banks have an opening, not before or after. The program sends candidates on interviews only when they are "job ready" and a good match for a particular position at the bank branch. A key factor boosting retention rates in the WINGS program is the postplacement support offered to participants and employers. Collaboration with the community college has simplified the bank's relations with government agencies and reduced the paperwork associated with the welfare-to-work initiative.

The examples presented here also illustrate some of the strategies deployed by specific programs to respond directly to industry concerns, such as substance abuse, absenteeism, and inappropriate workplace attitudes. The degree to which welfare-to-work programs provide basic and job-specific skills instruction varies by program, but all the programs in this study offer a combination of basic and vocational instruction at a level sufficient to be competitive in the job market. One of the key functions of the programs is screening candidates for job readiness, work attitudes, and functional basic and vocational skills required by the job. Once the students are successfully placed with an employer, most programs offer some postplacement services. The appropriateness of the community colleges' responses to welfare-to-work initiatives, in terms of implementing general workforce development programs, is ultimately defined by how well they are serving the needs of both students and employers.

Conclusions

The experience with welfare-to-work has tremendously advanced community colleges' ability to serve disadvantaged populations. In this context, welfare reform, and by implication workforce development programs for low-income or underrepresented students, have served to promote socioeconomic diversity on campuses. It is evident from the discussion in this chapter that community colleges initially responded to the 1996 welfare-to-work policy changes (PRWORA) by strengthening and transforming existing programs. Beyond this, many community colleges have created new, more advanced, and farsighted programs that position the institutions as regional labor market intermediaries. Given their experience with the welfare-to-work initiative and the prominent and favored role assigned to community colleges by the Workforce Investment Act, these institutions can capitalize on the restructuring of the federally funded employment system and act as primary providers of vocational training for adults and out-of-school youth.

Whether all community colleges can assume a prominent role in the emerging workforce development system will be determined by each institution's ability to transcend its focus on a traditional educational mission and expand to become a regional labor market intermediary. Indeed, community colleges that have evolved into the most significant labor intermediaries in their regions see themselves as playing a more comprehensive role than that of traditional educators. The community colleges selected for this study have a clear mission to link education with industry and have actively engaged in strategies to forge alliances and collaborations with employers, government agencies, employer associations, and community groups. For community colleges to become regional labor market intermediaries, they must learn from the ongoing experience other colleges have in developing welfare-to-work programs.

Recommendations to Community College Leadership

A key finding of this study is that community college leaders play a major role in the implementation of welfare-to-work programs. Policies and funding provide the opportunity for interventions, but teams of people within the colleges develop and sustain the programs. The following recommendations are based on our findings about what constitutes effective leadership practices. These recommendations include practical steps that have proven effective in colleges that have expanded existing or created new programs to serve welfare students.

Create a campuswide advisory board. Planning and developing welfare-to-work programs require the active participation of academic department leaders, program staff, instructors, and representatives from administration and support systems on campus. Formal or informal groups coordinating the college's efforts on a regular basis have a great impact in solving problems, minimizing conflicts, and expediting routine work.

Engage leaders of academic departments in the design of new programs and the redesign of old programs. Academic departments are the backbone of the community college system; without the active participation of department directors, any new initiative will be perceived as marginal, and implementation will become more difficult.

Design short-term vocational training programs as feeders to certificate programs, and certificate programs as feeders to degree programs. The forward articulation of short-term vocational courses conveys to students, staff, and faculty that the new vocational programs are spin-offs of existing academic programs. Articulation makes it possible for students to transfer to degree programs easily and create a path to career advancement.

Integrate basic education as part of all community college–based vocational training certificates. Basic education—the provision of functional literacy in English and mathematics at the college level—differentiates community college training from training provided by other institutions. A rigorous short-term training program gives colleges a competitive advantage in the market; students are better prepared for employment, and the program develops a reputation for producing high performers.

Target a specific sector for more effective short-term vocational training. A focus on a specific occupation within an industry helps providers target training methods and concentrate contacts for internships and placement in "hot" job fields. When short-term vocational training focuses on a specific sector, employers can develop a sense of ownership of the program and participate more actively in it.

Incorporate internships, work-study, cooperative work, and other work experience into the program. Supervised part-time work experience allows students to make a gradual transition to the workplace, helps them become socialized to the profession, and provides valuable work experience and positive role modeling.

Make job readiness training a part of regular programs, as all students in the community college can benefit from it. Job readiness courses designed for welfare-to-work participants include, among others, life and time management skills, interpersonal relations, workplace expectations, self-evaluation and self-motivation, and problem-solving and communication skills.

Incorporate workplace supports into program design during internships and after placement in full-time employment. Supporting trainees and employees in transition improves their chances of staying on the job after they begin working full time. Regular conferences with first-line supervisors resolve conflicts and minimize tensions before they become a problem.

Promote high-level partnerships with social and labor agencies and with community-based organizations. Building and maintaining relations with local government offices and community services agencies are necessary for the community college to position itself as a regional labor intermediary. Building relationships or partnerships essentially helps build links to jobs and complementary support services for students.

Develop better management and information systems to track welfare recipients and other targeted populations during and after program participation. Accurate information about students' profiles and their academic progress is an important planning and marketing tool that enables administrators to improve programs. Unfortunately, most college tracking systems fail to track basic program-related information and student characteristics over time.

Celebrate students' victories—big and small. It is important to recognize welfare-to-work and other disadvantaged students' achievements. Some of the programs reviewed in the study held regular graduation ceremonies and other activities to award certificates of achievement.

The accessibility and affordability of community colleges throughout the nation can have a great impact on the education of disadvantaged populations through workforce development efforts. Given their current advantageous position in regional labor markets, whether community colleges can become the primary providers of vocational training for adults and out-of-school youth will depend in part on their ability to transcend a traditional educational mission. From the results of this survey and case studies, it is clear that some community colleges have adopted a clear mission to link education with industry, and have engaged in successful strategies to forge alliances and collaborations with employers, government agencies, employer associations, and community groups to achieve such goals.

References

Bailey, T. "Integrating Vocational and Academic Education." In Mathematical Sciences Education Board of the National Research Council (ed.), *High School Mathematics at Work.* Washington, D.C.: National Academy Press, 1998.

Carnavale, A. P., and Desrochers, D. M. "The Role of Community Colleges in the New Economy. Spotlight on Education." *Community College Journal,* 1997, 67(5), 26–33.

Fisher, J. C. "Research on Adult Literacy Education in the Welfare-to-Work Transition." In L. G. Martin and J. C. Fisher (eds.), *The Welfare-to-Work Challenge for Adult Literacy Educators.* New Directions for Adult and Continuing Education, no. 83. San Francisco: Jossey-Bass, 1999.

Ganzglass, E. "Workforce Development and Welfare Block Grants: Implications for Community Colleges." *Community College Journal,* 1996, 66(4), 21–23.

Golonka, S., and Matus-Grossman, L. *Opening Doors: Expanding Educational Opportunities for Low-Income Workers.* New York and Washington, D.C.: MDRC and National Governors' Association, 2001.

Greenberg, M., Strawn, J., and Plimpton, L. *State Opportunities to Provide Access to Postsecondary. Education Under TANF.* Washington, D.C.: Center for Law and Social Policy, 1999.

Grubb, W. N. *Learning to Work: The Case for Reintegrating Job Training and Education.* New York: Russell Sage Foundation, 1996.

Grubb, W. N. "From Isolation to Integration: Occupational Education and the Emerging Systems of Workforce Development." *Centerpoint.* Berkeley: National Center for Research in Vocational Education, University of California, Berkeley, March 3, 1999.

Grubb, W. N., Badway, N., Bell, D., and Catellano, M. "Community Colleges and Welfare Reform: Emerging Practices, Enduring Problems." *Community College Journal,* 1999, 69(6), 30–36.

Grubb, W. N., and Associates. *Honored but Invisible: An Inside Look at Teaching in Community Colleges.* New York: Routledge, 1999.

Gueron, J. M., and Hamilton, G. *The Role of Education and Training in Welfare Reform.* Washington, D.C.: Brookings Institution, 2002.

Holzer, H. *What Employers Want: Job Prospects for Less-Educated Workers.* New York: Russell Sage Foundation, 1996.

Jenkins, D. S., and Fitzgerald, J. *Community Colleges: Connecting the Poor to Good Jobs.* Policy paper. Denver, Colo.: Center for Community College Policy, 1998.

Katsinas, S., Banachowski, G., Bliss, T. J., and Short, D.J.M. "Community College Involvement in Welfare-to-Work Programs." *Community College Journal of Research and Practice,* 1999, 23(4), 401–421.

Meléndez, E. *Working on Jobs: The Center for Employment Training.* Boston: Mauricio Gastón Institute, University of Massachusetts, 1996.

Meléndez, E., Falcón, L., and Bivens, J. "Community College Participation in Welfare Programs: Do State Policies Matter?" *Community College Journal of Research and Practice,* 2003, 27(3), 203–223.

Meléndez, E., and Harrison, B. "Matching the Disadvantaged to Job Opportunities: Structural Explanations for the Past Successes of the Center for Employment Training." *Economic Development Quarterly,* 1998, 12(1), 3–11.

Meléndez, E., and Suárez, C. "Opening College Doors for Disadvantaged Hispanics: An Assessment of Effective Programs and Practices." In R. Kazis and M. Miller (eds.), *Low Wage Workers in the New Economy.* Washington, D.C.: Urban Institute Press, 2001.

Meléndez, E., and others. *The Welfare-to-Work Policy Shock: How Community Colleges Are Addressing the Challenge.* New York: Community Development Research Center, 2002.

Moss, P., and Tilly, C. *Stories Employers Tell: Race, Skill, and Hiring in America.* New York: Russell Sage Foundation, 2001.

Perin, D. *Curriculum and Pedagogy to Integrate Occupational and Academic Instruction in the Community College: Implications for Faculty Development.* New York: Community College Research Center, Teachers College, Columbia University, 1998.

Salzman, H., Moss, P., and Tilly, C. *The New Corporate Landscape and Workforce Skills.* Stanford, Calif.: National Center for Postsecondary Improvement, School of Education, Stanford University, 1998.

Stokes, R. *Model Welfare-to-Work Initiatives in the United States: Effective Strategies for Moving TANF Recipients from Public Assistance to Self-Sufficiency.* Unpublished report prepared for the Connecticut Business and Industry Association by RSS Associates, 1996.

Strawn, J. *Beyond Job Search or Basic Education: Rethinking the Role of Skills in Welfare Reform.* Washington, D.C.: Center for Law and Social Policy, 1998.

EDWIN MELÉNDEZ is professor of management and urban policy at the Robert J. Milano Graduate School of Management and Urban Policy at the New School University in New York City.

LUIS M. FALCÓN is professor and associate provost, Northeastern University, Boston.

ALEXANDRA DE MONTRICHARD is a research associate at the Community Development Research Center at the Robert J. Milano Graduate School of Management and Urban Policy at the New School University in New York City.

6

This chapter compares the racial and ethnic diversity among faculty and academic leaders with that of the student population in two-year colleges. Using two national data sets, this study reveals that African American and Hispanic faculty and academic leaders remain underrepresented compared to the number of students of color attending the nation's two-year colleges.

Diversity in the Two-Year College Academic Workforce

Jerlando F. L. Jackson, L. Allen Phelps

Over the past decade the nation's two-year colleges have witnessed major shifts in diversity among students, faculty, and academic leaders (Astin, 1993; Bryant, 2001). Given the increasing and multifaceted role that diversity plays in two-year colleges, this chapter explores whether trends in hiring, retaining, and promoting people of color in the two-year academic workforce are keeping pace with trends in student enrollment. Using data from the 1993 and 1999 National Study of Postsecondary Faculty as well as the Integrated Postsecondary Education Data System, this chapter compares the proportional representation for people of color in faculty and academic leadership positions to students of color, and addresses the implications for policy and practice in two-year colleges. Because these data sets do not distinguish between two-year colleges and community colleges, all postsecondary institutions in this chapter will be referred to as two-year colleges.

Diversity in Two-Year Colleges

The nation's rapidly evolving demographics and changing economic and community contexts indicate that two-year colleges and their leaders have become increasingly important actors in addressing a number of educational, equity, and intercultural issues, as well as in supporting efforts to enhance economic and community development initiatives (Fujimoto, 1996; Opp and Gosetti, 2002; Vaughan, 1996). From an organizational perspective, two-year colleges can expose students to and engage them with diversity in three related ways (Gurin, Dey, Hurtado, and Gurin, 2002).

NEW DIRECTIONS FOR COMMUNITY COLLEGES, no. 127, Fall 2004 © Wiley Periodicals, Inc.

First, by attending or working in colleges with higher levels of racial or ethnic diversity, students, faculty, and academic leaders are exposed to *structural diversity,* which allows for new possibilities for teaching and learning. Second, the frequency and quality of intergroup interaction moves structural diversity experiences into the realm of *informal interactional diversity,* which often occurs outside classes in residence halls, student organizations, and social activities. Finally, *classroom diversity* engages faculty, staff, and students in learning and studying about diverse people and policies both within the curriculum and across two-year college programs.

Although by itself structural diversity is an insufficient condition for generating equitable learning opportunities and maximal educational benefits for all students (Gurin, Dey, Hurtado, and Gurin, 2002), it is nonetheless necessary to promote diversity among faculty in order to ensure positive learning outcomes for students of color (Opp, 2001; Opp and Gosetti, 2002). Because many academic leaders in two-year colleges are selected or recruited from faculty ranks, a diverse faculty is essential for advancing institutional efforts to achieve equitable and successful outcomes for all students.

Many empirical investigations have shown the benefits of diversity in two-year colleges. For example, using a national sample of 562 two-year institutions, Opp (2001) examined variables that predicted the presence of students of color at two-year colleges. He found that the strongest predictors of student diversity were the percentages of faculty and academic leaders of color and the amount of contact that students of color had with chief student affairs officers. This study suggests that a highly diverse academic workforce can promote institutional success and increase student diversity at two-year colleges. Opp's study, as well as the growing body of empirical and conceptual evidence of the importance of structural diversity in postsecondary institutions, underscores the importance of examining patterns of student, faculty, and academic leader diversity at two-year colleges.

Methodology

This chapter examines information from two national data sets and compares the proportion of faculty and academic leaders from certain races and ethnicities with that of students in two-year colleges in both 1993 and 1999. The following section describes the data sources, measures, and procedures used for these analyses.

Data Sources. This study utilized two primary data sources. First, it relied on the National Study of Postsecondary Faculty (NSOPF) surveys that were conducted by the National Center for Educational Statistics (NCES) during three academic years (1987–1988, 1992–1993, and 1998–1999) (U.S. Department of Education, 2002). Data from the 1992–1993 and 1998–1999 surveys were analyzed in order to track changes over time in the representation of faculty and academic leaders from diverse racial and ethnic backgrounds in two-year colleges. For this study, individuals who listed their principal function as teaching were categorized as faculty, and those who listed their principal function as administration were classified as academic leaders.

The second primary source used was the Integrated Postsecondary Education Data System (IPEDS) surveys administered by NCES. These surveys contain undergraduate enrollment data and were used to describe trends in postsecondary enrollment at institutional, state, and national levels. IPEDS data used in this study were derived from NCES *Enrollment in Higher Education* surveys from 1993 and 1999 (U.S. Department of Education, 2000).

Measures. The NSOPF data sets contain numerous variables that measure principal and primary activities for faculty in a variety of roles: teaching, administration, and research. This study focused on the variables contained in each data set that measured teaching and administrative assignments. Faculty who selected teaching as their principal activity represent the traditional role associated with faculty work. Faculty who selected administration as their principal activity generally held an administrative appointment in addition to their faculty role and, in most cases, filled limited-term academic leadership positions. From each NOSPF data set, a subset of executive-level leadership positions was also incorporated in this analysis. These positions include department chairs, deans, vice presidents, and provosts. NOSPF data were used to identify the race or ethnicity of individuals in faculty, academic leadership, and executive-level leadership positions. IPEDS enrollment counts were used to compute undergraduate enrollment data in two-year colleges.

Procedures. This study analyzed NSOPF and IPEDS data in order to track changes over time in the representation of faculty and academic leaders of different races and ethnicities, and compare those numbers to undergraduate student enrollment at two-year colleges. To examine trends across these data, descriptive statistics were calculated for all two-year colleges. In order to examine the levels of diversity among faculty and academic leaders in relation to student diversity, an equity measure was computed as well. Several scholars have suggested using equity measures in order to compare different levels of diversity in an institution. Yntema (1933) argued that an acceptable measure must be independent of the number of people in the distribution and the unit of measurement. Further, it must be a single value and easy to compute; it must also imply inequity and vary between set limits. The equity measure used in this study is the representation ratio.

The representation ratio summarizes the degree of inequity in an institution by calculating the proportion of students, faculty, and academic leaders of the same race or ethnicity (Cayer and Sigelman, 1980; Meier and Bohte, 2001). Representation ratios for individual racial or ethnic groups were computed by dividing the percentage of faculty or academic leaders from a certain race or ethnicity by the percentage of students from the same background in two-year colleges. For example, the ratio is equal to 1.0

when African Americans are represented in academic leadership positions at the same rate as in the student population. It is less than 1.0 when African Americans are underrepresented and greater than 1.0 when they are over-represented. The representation ratios presented in the next section were calculated using the aforementioned procedure, taking into account the sampling weights and stratification schema in each of the NSOPF and IPEDS surveys (U.S. Department of Education, 2000, 2002).

Results

The results of this study raise questions about the balance of faculty and academic leaders of color to students of color in U.S. two-year colleges. Figure 6.1 presents the representation ratios for students, faculty, and academic leaders in two-year colleges in both 1993 and 1999.

Faculty-to-Student Ratios. In 1993, whites filled 87.3 percent of two-year college faculty positions, whereas only 71 percent of the student body was white, which produced a representation ratio of 1.23. The rate of over-representation by white faculty increased to 1.33 in 1999, as the proportion of white students enrolled at two-year colleges declined from 71 to approximately 65 percent.

Conversely, the proportion of African American students enrolled at two-year colleges grew substantially between 1993 and 1999 (from 10.8 to 12.1 percent of the population), whereas the proportion of African American faculty increased only modestly (from 5.1 to 5.7 percent). During this six-year period, the representation ratio for African American faculty members remained at an alarmingly low level (below 0.50), meaning that many of the nation's African American two-year college students were not receiving instruction from faculty who looked like them.

Representation ratios for Hispanics—the fastest-growing student population—were equally distressing. IPEDS data reveal that between 1993 and 1996, the proportion of Hispanic students increased by nearly one-third, from 10.0 to 13.1 percent of the two-year college population. Unfortunately, in both years, Hispanic faculty constituted less than 5 percent of all two-year college faculty. The representation ratios for Hispanic faculty declined from 0.40 to 0.37, clearly indicating a significant gap in the college's ability to provide culturally relevant instruction to a rapidly growing Hispanic student population.

Representation ratios for the Asian American population are similarly dismal. Whereas the student population grew modestly between 1993 and 1999 from 5.3 percent to 6.4 percent of the two-year college population, the percentage of Asian American faculty stayed roughly the same, and thus the ratio of Asian American faculty to students dropped from 0.51 to 0.38. Significant attention must be given to increasing the numbers of Asian American, Hispanic, and African American faculty if the two-year professoriate is to accurately reflect the students of color being served.

Figure 6.1. Percent Distributions and Representation Ratios for Faculty, Students, and Academic Leaders by Race/Ethnicity at Two-Year Colleges

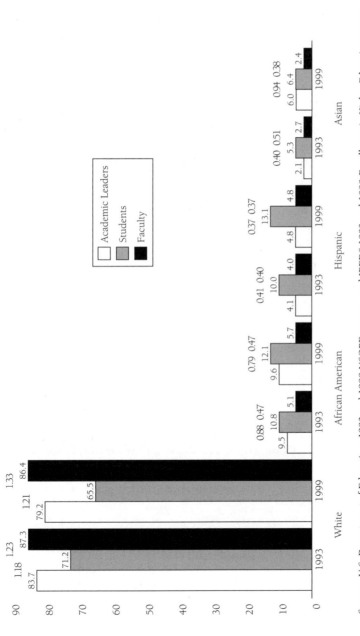

Sources: U.S. Department of Education, 1993 and 1999 NSOPF surveys, and IPEDS 1993 and 1999 *Enrollment in Higher Education* surveys.

Note: Employment counts for academic leadership positions were based on the number for each year: 24,867 in 1993 and 22,905 in 1999. Enrollment counts for undergraduate students were based on the number for each year: 14,305,000 in 1993 and 14,791,000 in 1999. Employment counts for faculty were based on the number for each year: 254,381 in 1993 and 209,759 in 1999.

Academic Leader–to–Student Ratios. Whites filled 83.7 percent of two-year college academic leadership positions in 1993, although only 71 percent of the student body was white. Thus the representation ratio was 1.18 in 1993 and increased to 1.21 by 1999. Although the proportion of African American students in two-year colleges grew substantially between 1993 and 1999, the proportion of African American academic leaders was virtually static. Thus the representation ratio for African American academic leaders declined slightly from 0.88 to 0.79. Because of this decline, substantial increases in the number of African American academic leaders are needed in order to achieve an equitable distribution.

Substantial increases in the number of Hispanic academic leaders are necessary as well, as the representation ratio of Hispanic academic leaders to students declined from 0.41 to 0.37 during this six-year period. In 1999, Hispanics made up only 4.8 percent of all academic leaders in two-year colleges, compared to 13.1 percent of all two-year college students. For Asian American students and academic leaders, however, the picture is somewhat brighter. In 1999, the representation ratio for these two groups was nearly balanced (0.94). It would appear that between 1993 and 1999, many efforts have been made to recruit or advance Asian Americans to academic leadership positions in the nation's two-year colleges.

Executive Leader–to–Student Ratios. As Table 6.1 shows, representation ratios and trends for two-year college executive-level leaders (that is, chairs, deans, vice presidents, and provosts) are in some cases similar to those for all academic leaders and in other cases very different. For example, representation ratios for white executive leaders are similar to academic leaders in both 1993 and 1999, and demonstrate substantial overrepresentation. Trends for Asian American executive leaders followed that of Asian American academic leaders as well; the representation ratio for this group increased from 0.62 to 1.38. Interestingly, Asian American executives became overrepresented in two-year colleges during this time period, and exceeded the proportion of white executives in 1999.

Table 6.1. Comparisons of Representation Ratios for Academic Leaders and Executive-Level Leaders at Two-Year Colleges

	Academic Leaders		Executive-Level Leaders	
	1993 (n = 24,867)	1999 (n = 22,905)	1993 (n = 9,409)	1999 (n = 8,380)
White	1.18	1.21	1.28	1.18
African American	0.88	0.79	0.44	0.64
Hispanic	0.41	0.37	0.09	0.37
Asian	0.40	0.94	0.62	1.38

Source: U.S. Department of Education, 1993 and 1999 NSOPF surveys.

African American executive leaders, however, did not follow the same pattern as African American academic leaders. Rather, the representation ratio for African American executive leaders increased between 1993 and 1999 (from 0.44 to 0.64). Hispanic executives showed a similar pattern: the representation ratio for this group increased from 0.09 to 0.37 during this six-year time period. Although substantial gains were made in advancing African American and Hispanic individuals to executive-level leadership positions, significant gaps remain, as these groups have achieved only 64 percent and 37 percent of the equity parity implied in the representation ratio measure.

Discussion and Implications

As the nation's two-year colleges confront the challenges of serving an increasingly diverse and rapidly changing student population, the development and retention of academic leaders and faculty of color are essential for advancing the capacity of these institutions to deliver high-quality instructional programs. To ensure that all students benefit from advising, support, teaching, learning, and career and educational planning provided by faculty and academic leaders of color, it is imperative that extended efforts be made to develop, recruit, and retain these individuals in leadership roles. The results discussed in this chapter provide a national perspective on the balance between two-year college students of color and faculty, academic, and executive leaders of color.

Three major findings arose from this study. First, between 1993 and 1999, two-year colleges enrolled an increasingly diverse student population, but made uneven gains in diversifying the academic workforce. Although the increasing numbers of faculty and academic leaders of color will help two-year colleges successfully educate students of color, substantial and sustained efforts are still needed to develop both faculty and academic leaders of color in the future. Some steps have been taken in this direction. Through collaborative efforts between two-year colleges and state higher education authorities, several states have launched leadership development programs over the past decade. Minnesota's Leadership Academy (http://www.education.umn.edu/wcfe/LeadershipAcademy) and Iowa's Leadership Institute for a New Century (http://www.educ.iastate.edu/elps/hged/lincdes.htm), for example, have placed an explicit priority on serving women and people of color working in two-year colleges. Using a cohort-based approach, participants are engaged in weekend seminars, internships, distance learning interactions, and in-depth field studies leading to advanced degrees in the field of higher education. Bragg's recent description of ten university-based community college leadership programs (2002) indicates that diversity courses and experiences are recent additions to the curriculum. To date, unfortunately, systematic evidence has not been compiled on the implementation and effects of these programs, but the Web sites indicate that non-white and female students are highly represented among all participants as well as among those who complete the program. Through program assessments as well as bench-marking studies, state-level and institution-level leaders should examine the effectiveness and impact of leadership development programs for administrators and faculty of color in other states, and launch similar efforts.

Second, although gains have been made in Hispanic and African American attainment of academic leadership positions, these groups are still significantly underrepresented at two-year colleges. Therefore, two-year colleges should continue to recruit faculty and academic leaders of color and encourage them to enter leadership development programs. As well, universities and state higher education agencies should continue to recruit prospective leaders from Hispanic and African American communities. In addition, national professional associations (such as the American Association of Community Colleges [AACC] and the League for Innovation in the Community College), in collaboration with leadership development programs with a state-level or institution-specific focus, should consider the following recruitment, training, and development strategies:

Develop partnerships with scholars of higher education or educational administration in Historically Black Colleges and Universities and Hispanic-Serving Institutions in order to develop new programs, institutes, or seminars aimed at improving faculty and administrative leadership diversity in two-year colleges

Create culturally focused mentoring programs that enable new African American and Hispanic administrators and faculty members in two-year colleges to work closely with highly accomplished faculty and administrative leaders from similar cultural backgrounds

Establish advanced study fellowships for non-white graduate students enrolled in community college leadership development programs

Expand AACC's and the League for Innovation in the Community College's leadership development initiatives to create seminars and information campaigns that provide national and regional strategies for filling the significant diversity gaps in the nation's two-year postsecondary academic workforce

The third major finding in this chapter is that two-year colleges have made more substantial gains in diversifying executive-level leadership than academic leadership. Greater representation of people of color among top-level administrative positions indicates a more equitable distribution of key leadership positions at the nation's two-year colleges. However, organizational and personnel strategies used to make these important gains should be identified and carefully studied in order to identify promising practices and innovative policies that could be used to make improvements in other positions within the two-year colleges' academic workforce. According to Bowen and Muller (1996), key recommendations for advancing administrative diversity in two-year colleges include the following:

Develop and publicize college diversity goals
Use clear policies and procedures for hiring, awarding tenure, and evaluating performance
Employ consulting organizations that specialize in minority recruitment
Publicize openings in minority community publications
Search for administrative candidates from sources other than the traditional academic pipeline (for example, public schools or the military)
Encourage minority faculty to participate in academic leadership activities

Conclusion

Historically, two-year colleges have provided an array of educational opportunities and programs to a very diverse population (Opp, 2002) and are widely acknowledged as a key component of systematic efforts to broaden access and diversity in higher education. Faculty and academic leaders of color play very important roles in ensuring access and success for students of color in two-year colleges. As Opp (2001) suggests, colleges with higher percentages of faculty and administrators of color are more likely to attract a greater proportion of students of color, which in turn contributes to a campus climate that is more tolerant and supportive of diversity. This analysis demonstrates that although faculty and academic leaders of color—especially those in executive-level positions—are gaining representation in two-year colleges, there is still much work that needs to be done to make our colleges warm, welcoming, and inclusive campus environments that better serve diverse constituencies.

References

Astin, A. W. "Diversity and Multiculturalism on Campus: How Are Students Affected?" *Change*, 1993, 25(2), 44–49.
Bowen, R. C., and Muller, G. H. (ed.). *Achieving Administrative Diversity*. New Directions for Community Colleges, no. 94. San Francisco: Jossey-Bass, 1996.
Bragg, D. D. "Doing Their Best: Exemplary Graduate Leadership Programs." *Community College Journal*, 2002, 73(1), 49–53.
Bryant, A. N. "Community College Students: Recent Findings and Trends." *Community College Review*, 2001, 29(3), 77–94.
Cayer, N. J., and Sigelman, L. "Minorities and Women in State and Local Government: 1973–1975." *Public Administration Review*, 1980, 40, 442–450.
Fujimoto, M. J. "The Community College Presidency: An Asian Pacific American Perspective." In R. C. Bowen and G. H. Muller (eds.), *Achieving Administrative Diversity*. New Directions for Community Colleges, no. 94. San Francisco: Jossey-Bass, 1996.
Gurin, P., Dey, E. L., Hurtado, S., and Gurin, G. "Diversity and Higher Education: Theory and Impact on Educational Outcomes." *Harvard Educational Review*, 2002, 72(3), 330–366.
Meier, K. J., and Bohte, J. "Structure and Discretion: Missing Links in Representative Bureaucracy." *Journal of Public Administration Research and Theory*, 2001, 11, 455–470.

Opp, R. D. "Enhancing Recruitment Success for Two-Year College Students of Color." *Community College Journal of Research and Practice,* 2001, *25*(2), 71–87.

Opp, R. D. "Enhancing Program Completion Rates Among Two-Year College Students of Color." *Community College Journal of Research and Practices,* 2002, *26*(2), 147–163.

Opp, R. D., and Gosetti, P. P. "Equity for Women Administrators of Color in Two-Year Colleges: Progress and Prospects." *Community College Journal of Research and Practice,* 2002, *26*(7–8), 591–608.

U.S. Department of Education, National Center for Education Statistics. *Enrollment in Higher Education.* Washington, D.C.: U.S. Department of Education, National Center for Education Statistics, 2000.

U.S. Department of Education, National Center for Education Statistics. *1999 National Study of Postsecondary Faculty (NSOPF: 99) Methodology Report.* Washington, D.C.: U.S. Department of Education, National Center for Education Statistics, 2002.

Vaughan, G. B. "Paradox and Promise: Leadership and the Neglected Minorities." In R. C. Bowen and G. H. Muller (eds.), *Achieving Administrative Diversity.* New Directions for Community Colleges, no. 94. San Francisco: Jossey-Bass, 1996.

Yntema, D. "Measures of Inequality in the Personal Distribution of Wealth or Income." *American Statistical Association Journal,* 1933, *28*, 423–433.

JERLANDO F. L. JACKSON is assistant professor of higher and postsecondary education and faculty associate for the Wisconsin Center for the Advancement of Postsecondary Education at the University of Wisconsin-Madison.

L. ALLEN PHELPS is a professor of educational leadership and policy analysis and director of the Center on Education and Work at the University of Wisconsin-Madison.

This chapter describes the organization, operations, and goals of the Alliance for Equity in Higher Education, a national coalition of associations and institutions founded to serve the emerging majority of racially diverse college students.

The Alliance for Equity in Higher Education

Jamie P. Merisotis, Katherine A. Goulian

The Alliance for Equity in Higher Education (Alliance) was founded to foster collaboration and mutual goal setting for minority higher education following the reauthorization of the Higher Education Act in 1998. Agreeing that cooperation rather than competition over limited federal funding would significantly expand educational opportunities for students of color, the leaders of the American Indian Higher Education Consortium (AIHEC), the Hispanic Association of Colleges and Universities (HACU), and the National Association for Equal Opportunity in Higher Education (NAFEO) joined together in 1999 in an alliance that marked an important turning point for minority education. The Alliance serves as a means of working collaboratively and speaking with one voice to better serve the needs of racially diverse students. The Alliance declared several goals, including establishing common public policy objectives, enhancing policymakers' as well as the public's understanding of the vital roles played by the two- and four-year Minority-Serving Institutions, and improving communication among the various organizations and institutions.

Alliance Member Organizations

The three Alliance member organizations collectively represent 340 colleges and universities and educate approximately one-third of all African American, American Indian, and Hispanic students enrolled in U.S. higher education. The Institute for Higher Education Policy (IHEP) coordinates activities for the Alliance members. The following are brief overviews of each of the member organizations of the Alliance and their constituencies.

AIHEC. Founded in 1972 as an informal collaboration by the presidents of the nation's first six tribal community colleges, AIHEC currently represents thirty-four tribal community colleges and universities in the United States and one in Canada. AIHEC's mission is to support the work of Tribal Colleges and Universities (TCUs) and the national movement for tribal self-determination. AIHEC assists in maintaining standards of high-quality education, developing an accrediting body for two- and four-year institutions serving American Indian populations, and reaching out to other national education organizations. It promotes and supports the development of new TCUs and advocates for national policy, legislation, and regulations to strengthen American Indian higher education. AIHEC also promotes opportunities for TCUs in science and information technology (IT), agriculture and natural resources use, and pre-K–12 linkages (American Indian Higher Education Consortium, 2000).

HACU. Founded in 1986 as an advocacy group to promote the educational attainment of Hispanic students and support nationally recognized Hispanic-Serving Institutions (HSIs), HACU has more than three hundred U.S. and international two- and four-year member institutions with high concentrations of Hispanic students (Laden, 2004). More than half of HACU's members are HSIs according the federal definition that requires at least 25 percent full-time equivalent (FTE) Hispanic enrollment. HACU's guidelines define HSIs more broadly, however, and include all institutions with 25 percent Hispanic student enrollment by *head count*, rather than by FTE. HACU's broader definition will be used throughout the remainder of this chapter.

HACU member institutions are located in twenty-one states and Puerto Rico, and its associate members are in six Spanish-speaking countries. Overall, U.S. HACU member institutions educate two out of every three Hispanics enrolled in U.S. higher education (http://www.msi-alliance.org).

NAFEO. The oldest of the Alliance member organizations, NAFEO represents 118 Historically Black Colleges and Universities (HBCUs)—America's oldest special-mission institutions—as well as other predominantly black two- and four-year institutions. NAFEO has worked since its inception in 1969 to raise awareness of HBCUs, to implement programs and policies that support black and other minority students, and to increase black enrollment in HBCUs. NAFEO institutions enroll 370,000 students, or one-third of all black undergraduate, graduate, and professional students (National Association for Equal Opportunity in Higher Education, 2004).

Minority-Serving Institutions

The Alliance has made collaboration among institutions that serve racially diverse students an increasingly popular concept and has promoted the concept of Minority-Serving Institutions. The term comes from the monograph

Minority-Serving Institutions: Distinct Purposes, Common Goals (Merisotis and O'Brien, 1998), which explored the emerging possibility of a common policy for HBCUs, TCUs, and HSIs. The term *Minority-Serving Institutions* emerged during the writing of the monograph as a way to refer collectively to these three groups of institutions. The term was modeled after the definition of Hispanic-Serving Institutions, which had been recognized by federal law just four years earlier.

The term *Minority-Serving Institutions* has become integrated into the higher education lexicon. To illustrate, aside from the authors' use of the term in this volume, an Internet search for the term identified more than fifteen hundred Web documents, suggesting that it is well-established and commonly used. The Alliance refers to the combined institutions represented by AIHEC, HACU, and NAFEO as Minority-Serving Institutions (MSIs).

As of 2000, approximately 1.8 million students (11 percent) were enrolled in MSIs (Alliance for Equity in Higher Education, 2003); 57 percent (194) of the MSIs are four-year colleges, and 43 percent (146) are two-year colleges. Two-thirds are public, and one-third are private nonprofit institutions. These MSIs confer 21 percent of all college degrees and certificates and nearly 50 percent of teacher education degrees awarded to students. The increasing number of minority students in institutions of higher education is reflected in the growing enrollment in all three of the Alliance's member institutions, and particularly in community colleges, which have traditionally been critical in enrolling minority college students. MSIs have also grown at faster rates than other colleges and universities; enrollment in MSIs increased an average of 22 percent between 1990 and 2000, whereas the overall rate of enrollment growth in U.S. institutions was only 9 percent (Alliance for Equity in Higher Education, 2003).

Alliance Projects

There are a growing number of programs, projects, and initiatives that emphasize the benefits of partnering among MSIs. For example, the Advanced Networking for Minority-Serving Institutions project (http://www. anmsi.org) was developed by Educause to provide increased technology infrastructure capacity. The USA Funds–supported initiative called Project Equality and Accountability examined new public policy options for addressing student loan default rates at MSIs (http://www.usafunds.org/News/ dpdm125.pdf). The Building Engagement and Attainment of Minority Students (BEAMS) project—sponsored jointly by the American Association for Higher Education and the National Survey of Student Engagement—is aimed at improving student retention and achievement at MSIs (http://www. iub.edu/~nsse/html/beams_feature.htm). Further, numerous federal agency programs support scientific and other academic programs at MSIs, including the Model Institutions of Excellence Program (http://www. mieprogram.

org), which is sponsored as a collaborative of the National Science Foundation and the National Aeronautics and Space Administration.

The Kellogg Program. In 2002 the Alliance received a four-year, $6 million grant from the W. K. Kellogg Foundation to launch the Kellogg MSI Leadership Fellows Program. The grant was designed to help train the next generation of presidents and other senior-level leaders at MSIs and to retain the talent pool of current and future leaders at these institutions (http://www.msi-alliance.org).

The Kellogg MSI Leadership Fellows Program focuses on the interaction of the institution, the individual leader, and the culturally unique and complex situations endemic to MSIs, *as well as* individual leadership development. AIHEC, HACU, and NAFEO each administers its own distinct program to meet its specific needs. Each of the three programs is overseen by its own independent advisory board of current and former leaders at two- and four-year MSIs. The purpose of each program is to prepare ten exemplary individuals per year (that is, thirty individuals across the three programs) for the challenges and rigors of assuming senior-level leadership positions at two- and four-year MSIs. Kellogg Fellows participate in joint Alliance and individual member workshops, seminars, and discussion groups during the academic year. Fellows also have mentors who are presidents at other MSIs.

Other critical activities include bringing together expert groups twice per year to provide the Alliance with ongoing guidance on substantive issues related to the collaborative agendas of its members. Experts from two- and four-year campuses and the broader MSI community provide guidance to the Alliance on teacher education, technology, and research and policy analysis; help shape public policy recommendations; and promote greater understanding of the unique issues and concerns of MSIs.

Reauthorization of the Higher Education Act. In 2003, the Alliance announced joint recommendations concerning the next reauthorization of the Higher Education Act (HEA, http://www.msi-alliance.org/csc/cscdocs/February2003.htm). This effort demonstrated the progress achieved by Alliance members in a relatively short period of time. The 2003 HEA reauthorization recommendations were aimed at establishing an influential voice for MSIs in the Higher Education Act in the coming years. These recommendations and the collaborative efforts of the Alliance were positively received by policymakers and education leaders. The Alliance's HEA recommendations included doubling the amount of the authorized maximum Pell grant and providing opportunities for MSI participation in various federal programs by assuring MSI applications of an equal playing field with current grant recipients. Another recommendation involved significantly increasing authorization levels under Title III and Title V to ensure the continued growth and development of MSIs. Additionally, a graduate fellowship program was recommended to improve the prospects of MSI graduates and other minorities seeking to enter the higher education professoriate.

Lastly, the Alliance recommended strengthening Title VI to enhance opportunities for MSIs to participate in curriculum abroad (Alliance for Equity in Higher Education, 2003).

In sum, these recommendations were extremely important to the future of both minority students and the Alliance. First, the joint recommendations established common public policy objectives for Alliance member organizations, marking achievement of one of the key goals identified at the time of the Alliance's formation. The recommendations also united all three members in a large piece of federal legislation and allowed them to speak with one voice instead of three disjointed or conflicting voices. Finally, these recommendations set a precedent for collaboration and cooperation, and helped to jointly promote the access, retention, and success of racially diverse two- and four-year students.

Public Policy Agenda

In its first four years, the Alliance accomplished a number of goals, especially in the public policy arena. Beyond the specific goal of developing HEA reauthorization recommendations, the Alliance's public policy agenda has emphasized two themes: eliminating the technology gap between disadvantaged and more well-off students and institutions; and reducing the performance gap between minority and white students. This theme includes issues of teacher preparation, remedial education, first-generation status, and testing. The Alliance's two themes have guided its public policy efforts and, along with work by technology and teacher education expert groups, have led to other actions, including testimony at Senate hearings, letters to Capitol Hill regarding appropriations, and other communications seeking to influence federal decisions impacting MSIs.

The Alliance's current federal policy agenda continues to advocate the recommendations outlined in the Alliance's HEA reauthorization recommendations, and meanwhile its member organizations have and are pursuing several other mutually beneficial policies. For example, the Alliance was a major proponent of the Minority-Serving Institution Digital and Wireless Technology Opportunity Act that was approved by the Senate in 2003. This legislation provides important support for MSIs to enhance their technology capacities and thereby produce graduates better able to meet the nation's growing demand for a highly skilled, technologically proficient workforce (Alliance for Equity in Higher Education, 2003).

The Alliance is also engaged in much research about and for MSIs. For example, although some information had been gathered about HBCUs, TCUs, and HSIs as distinct institutions, the lack of research on the newly unified community of the three members led to several papers and major policy reports that explore MSI issues. The Alliance's first major policy report, *Educating the Emerging Majority* (2000), examined the roles that MSIs play and the challenges they face in educating teachers of color. The report recommended public policy reforms and proposed solutions to address the teacher shortage. It also recommended that quality assessments of teacher education programs be based on a diverse set of factors rather than on single measures that can have a disproportionate impact on institutions that educate large numbers of minority teachers.

Another major policy report from the Alliance (2004) examined the changing ways in which technology is used at MSIs. This report combined a survey of MSIs with profiles of campuses that have excelled in the application of technology for teaching and learning, administrative, and other purposes. Increased investment in MSI technology capacity was supported in the report as a means of ensuring that MSIs are not trapped in a perpetual catch-up situation in comparison to majority institutions.

Future Plans

At a retreat held in 2003, Alliance members reviewed the first four years of accomplishments and discussed the Alliance's future agenda. Alliance member organizations noted that they have kept their pledge to change the face of "business as usual" in higher education policy. As a next step, the Alliance seeks to deliver much more through proactive activities and fundraising designed to make permanent the Alliance's role, aims, and objectives. Local, state, and federal policy agendas for the future prioritize educating globally aware leaders; creating access to technology; improving information and research about MSIs; improving teacher education; and involving minority students in international programs.

Leadership. In addition to the Kellogg MSI Leadership Fellows Program, the Alliance is pursuing two other leadership development initiatives. One is a New Presidents Academy, a fee-based seminar approximately one week in length for new presidents of two- and four-year MSIs. The New Presidents Academy will include some overlap with the curriculum of the Kellogg MSI Leadership Fellows Program but will be tailored to the immediate practical concerns of new presidents. The other is a student leadership network that will include a meeting of campus-based student organizations to build cross-community collaboration and understanding.

Technology. The Alliance submitted a major proposal to the National Science Foundation to support a Phase II of the Advanced Networking with Minority-Serving Institutions project, which is currently housed at Educause. Phase II represents an opportunity for the Alliance to assume ownership of the project and will include technical assistance, training, education programs to support IT, and communications systems to strengthen IT staff capacities.

Research and Policy Analysis. More research is necessary to make the case for investment in MSIs. One major research project involves describing the academic capacities of MSIs and identifying where Alliance institutions do well (such as in teacher education) despite underinvestment of funds in programs and where MSIs have more limited capacities (such as in science, mathematics, and engineering) despite the clear societal need for more and better trained individuals in those fields. This research draws from analyses of federal IPEDS data, a survey of MSIs, and analyses of U.S. Department of Labor data regarding future labor force needs.

The Alliance also supports and endorses redefining quality and standards of student success; comparing investment in MSIs and analyzing how their financial capacities contribute to the public good; investigating the history of minority higher education at TCUs, HBCUs, and HSIs; recruiting and retaining minority faculty; and describing MSIs' future contributions and visions for supporting the nation's economic, social, and cultural development.

Teacher Education. Although the Alliance's HEA reauthorization recommendations called for federal support for teacher education at MSIs, the Alliance itself is also making teacher education a major priority. Plans to improve teacher education include activities that increase institutional capacity, promote collaboration across MSIs, and pilot-test innovations that go beyond current models of teacher education. A major part of this plan will focus on educating science, computer science, and mathematics teachers. According to the *Educating the Emerging Minority* report (2000), a number of MSI community colleges are already offering teacher education programs. As Townsend and Ignash (2003) note, some of these programs allow students to concurrently earn their bachelor's degree; in others students can enroll in transfer programs articulated to preservice teacher programs in nearby universities.

International Programs. The Alliance has increased efforts to involve more minority students and faculty in major international programs (such as the Fulbright Association) and to encourage presidents and other leaders of institutions to be attuned to the growing global context of higher education, especially in the Americas. As a first step, an expert group will advise the Alliance on international education issues and priorities for MSIs. The Alliance will also convene a meeting where two- and four-year MSI presidents and other institutional leaders can speak with those who manage major international programs in either the federal government or private sectors.

Conclusion

The overarching goal of the Alliance is to better serve the increasing number of racially and ethnically diverse students who attend MSIs by continuing to forge a strong bond among the three member organizations. MSIs play a critical role in providing access to and supporting the retention and academic success of disadvantaged students and, as highlighted in other chapters in this volume, they stand on the front lines in educating the nation's emerging majority populations. There is no question that HBCUs, HSIs, and TCUs are integral to the country's continued social and economic development and to realizing the potential and promise of every individual. The Alliance for Equity in Higher Education is committed to ensuring that *all* Americans are able to aspire to, pursue, and benefit from a college education and thereby contribute to the nation's economic competitiveness, social stability, and cultural richness.

References

Alliance for Equity in Higher Education. *Educating the Emerging Majority: The Role of Minority-Serving Colleges and Universities in Confronting America's Teacher Crisis.* Washington, D.C.: Institute for Higher Education Policy, 2000.

Alliance for Equity in Higher Education. "Policy Priorities for the Higher Education Act Reauthorization." Unpublished position paper, 2003.

Alliance for Equity in Higher Education. *Serving the Nation: Opportunities and Challenges in the Use of Information Technology at Minority-Serving Colleges and Universities.* Washington, D.C.: Institute for Higher Education Policy, 2004.

American Indian Higher Education Consortium. "Mission Statement, 2000." 2000. http://www.aihec.org/mission.htm. Accessed June 3, 2004.

Laden, B. V. "Hispanic-Serving Institutions: What Are They? Where Are They?" *Community College Journal of Research and Practice,* 2004, *28*(3), 181–198.

Merisotis, J., and O'Brien, C. (eds.). *Minority-Serving Institutions: Distinct Purposes, Common Goals.* New Directions for Higher Education, no. 102. San Francisco: Jossey-Bass, 1998.

National Association for Equal Opportunity in Higher Education. "About NAFEO." http://www.nafeo.org/index3.html. Accessed June 3, 2004.

Townsend, B. K., and Ignash, J. "Community College Roles in Teacher Education: Current Approaches and Future Possibilities." In B. K. Townsend and J. Ignash (eds.), *The Role of the Community College in Teacher Education.* New Directions in Community Colleges, no. 121. San Francisco: Jossey-Bass, 2003.

JAMIE P. MERISOTIS *is president of the Institute for Higher Education Policy in Washington, D.C.*

KATHERINE A. GOULIAN *is a research assistant at the American Institutes for Research.*

8

This chapter summarizes useful and relevant resources and information on the topic of serving minority populations in community colleges, and presents information about several programs and services that have been successful in ensuring minority student success.

Resources and Information for Serving Minority Populations

Victor Sáenz

U.S. community colleges have long been regarded as beacons of access and educational opportunity for the masses, and at no time has this function been more critical than at the present. Community colleges have successfully adapted to waves of societal changes over the last century, yet currently a unique combination of demographic and enrollment shifts is challenging the resiliency of these open-access institutions in serving an increasingly diverse population (Schuetz, 2002).

This chapter serves as a synthesis of relevant resources and critical information on the topic of serving minority populations in community colleges. Of special note is that a majority of the resources highlighted in this chapter are readily available through the ERIC database, now accessible at its new online home at http://www.eduref.org/Eric. Drawing on material presented earlier in this volume, this chapter will provide information and relevant resources on demographic and enrollment trends in two-year institutions, minority degree completion, the community college transfer function, Minority-Serving Institutions (MSIs), and campus racial climate issues. It will then present selected programs and services that facilitate greater minority student success.

As has been acknowledged throughout this volume, trends in demographics, enrollment, persistence, and transfer highlight the increasing importance of community colleges as vital gateways to higher education for

---

Many of the LACCD programs and services presented in the last section of this chapter were drawn from a list compiled by Linda Serra Hagedorn.

racially and ethnically diverse students. As minority students arrive in increasing numbers at their doorsteps, community colleges must strive to better serve their emerging majority populations so as not to dampen these students' long-term prospects for educational attainment and success.

Community College Demographics

Several national databases contain information about community college demographics. One important resource is the U.S. Department of Education's National Center for Education Statistics (NCES), which offers a vast array of historical data that enable users to explore long-range trends in postsecondary education. In NCES's annual *Digest of Education Statistics* (http://nces.ed.gov/programs/digest/d02), data on enrollment trends at two- and four-year institutions are disaggregated by gender, race or ethnicity, institutional type (that is, two- or four-year colleges), and institutional control (public or private institutions).

The American Council on Education's annual reports on minorities in higher education are also useful resources for demographic data on minority students in postsecondary education. The most recent report, titled *Minorities in Higher Education 2002–2003, Twentieth Annual Status Report* (http://www.acenet.edu/bookstore/pubInfo.cfm?pubID=234), synthesizes data from NCES, the U.S. Census Bureau (http://www.census.gov), and the U.S. Equal Employment Opportunity Commission (http://www.eeoc.gov) in compiling a portrait of trends and indicators for minority students across secondary and postsecondary educational sectors. Among the many relevant findings in this report, the authors noted a 143 percent increase in the number of associate degrees awarded to minority students between 1980 and 2000, which mirrors similar trends in enrollment growth during the same period. The annual report is widely recognized as an important national source of information on current trends related to minorities in higher education.

Minority Student Degree Completion

Even as enrollments continue to surge at two-year institutions, minority student degree completion rates remain low, and transfer rates to four-year colleges and universities are even lower. Of the two hundred thousand associate degrees awarded by community colleges in 2000, only 9.6 percent went to African Americans, 10.1 percent to Hispanics, 5.3 percent to Asian Americans and Pacific Islanders, and 1 percent to American Indians or Alaska Natives (U.S. Department of Education, 2002). All these figures are lower than the racial groups' proportional representation in the student body. Data on minority student degree completion can be accessed through the NCES publication *Profiles of Undergraduates in U.S. Postsecondary Institutions: 1999–2000* (U.S. Department of Education, 2002). Other organizations such as the National Collegiate Athletic Association (http://www.ncaa.org), the ACT (http://www.act.org), and the Education Trust (http://www.edtrust.org) also publish data on minority student degree completion rates, although these reports primarily focus on four-year institutions.

The Transfer Function

Although there is general consensus that transfer rates from two-year institutions have recently declined among all student groups, limitations in available data as well as continuing controversy over how best to measure transfer rates make it difficult to define precisely the extent or causes of the decline (Wassmer, Moore, and Shulock, 2003). Nonetheless, research on transfer students is available, and ranges from discussions about the best rubric for defining and measuring transfer rates (Bradburn and Hurst, 2001) to more in-depth analyses of such issues as student satisfaction, academic performance, and patterns in the transfer process (Kozeracki, 2001; Townsend, 2001). Recent studies estimate that although the overall transfer rate is currently somewhere between 20 and 25 percent (Bryant, 2001), disparities in transfer rates persist across racial and ethnic groups, even among students most likely to transfer (Wassmer, Moore, and Shulock, 2003).

These findings highlight the importance of supporting the transfer function through more "academic" curricula, greater faculty involvement in the transfer function, more effective institutional research, better articulation policies with four-year institutions, and substantial support and advising services for students (Cuseo, 1998). To explore more information and research on the transfer function of community colleges, see Laanan's New Directions for Community Colleges volume titled *Transfer Students: Trends and Issues* (2001), the Education Commission of the States' publication *Transfer and Articulation Policies* (2001), and the California Postsecondary Education Commission's report *Student Transfer in California Postsecondary Education* (2002).

Minority-Serving Institutions

Higher education institutions are challenged to acknowledge changes in demographic trends while still responding proactively to the persistent issues of access, retention, graduation, transfer, campus climate, and faculty and staff diversity (Rendón, 2003). Many community colleges are already recognizing and responding to the academic, co-curricular, and cultural needs of their increasingly diverse student populations, and this volume has served to spotlight some of the lessons learned. In particular, urban colleges and MSIs are uniquely and critically positioned at the forefront of efforts to increase the success of minority students. Specific information on MSIs can be found in the U.S. Department of Education report *Accredited Postsecondary Minority Institutions* (2003).

MSIs are especially important to serving minority populations, as they enroll high proportions of low-income, minority, and educationally disadvantaged students. Federal policymakers have acknowledged the critical role MSIs play by targeting federal funds for institutional development. This funding stream, initially established through the 1998 reauthorization of the Higher Education Act (http://www.ed.gov/offices/OPE/PPI/Reauthor/index.html), has continued to increase since the initial appropriation. The U.S. Department of Housing and Urban Development (HUD) has also begun to pay more attention to MSIs. In January 2003, HUD released a report titled *Minority-Serving Institutions of Higher Education: Developing Partnerships to Revitalize Communities* (http://www.oup.org/pubs/minority-report.pdf). This report details and celebrates the accomplishments of MSIs participating in one of HUD's four programs that support long-term partnerships aimed at improving life in urban neighborhoods and local communities.

The emergence of MSIs has initiated various organizational and institutional alliances aimed at harnessing resources to service minority populations and achieve minority student success. For instance, Chapter Seven of this volume discusses the Alliance for Equity in Higher Education, a policy-based coalition that promotes greater collaboration and cooperation among MSIs in order to create greater access and opportunities in higher education and to recognize and preserve cultural diversity for emerging majority students.

Racial Culture and Climate

The increasing numbers of racially and ethnically diverse students at community colleges have compelled faculty and administrators to rethink their traditional modes of teaching and learning and to explore new ways to ensure that institutional access, academic success, and equal opportunity for social and career mobility are available and culturally appropriate for all students. Evident in many community colleges is an effort to shape the instructional and institutional climate of campuses and classrooms in a way that supports individual and cultural differences in learning styles, value systems, and educational preferences (Kezar and Eckel, 2000; Szelenyi, 2001).

Another institutional effort to increase the numbers of minority students in community colleges is the development of culturally relevant retention services. Historically, strategies for improving student retention have been crafted around the profile of a "traditional" college student (one who starts college right after high school, is financially dependent on parents, attends college full time, lives on campus, and has few work or family obligations), yet a number of community college faculty and leaders have recognized that retention strategies based on the traditional student are less applicable at community colleges and MSIs (Rendón, 2000). Thus many community colleges and MSIs have begun to tailor retention strategies to the needs and realities of current community college students, many of whom are from diverse racial and ethnic backgrounds, are older, and attend part time. The next section will profile a selection of programs and services that are aimed at serving minority student populations.

Programs and Services Serving Minority Populations

The following programs and services are aimed at facilitating greater educational attainment and success for minority community college students. These abbreviated listings and the brief descriptions and information contained in them are not intended to be exhaustive or comprehensive. To obtain complete contact information, follow the Web link and contact the program and service offices directly.

Academic Programs and Services

The following resources provide information and examples of effective academic programs and services aimed at minority students.

• **Bridges to the Future, National Institutes of Health (NIH).** A national initiative of the NIH, the Bridges program is dedicated to developing a pool of minority students to become tomorrow's leaders in biomedical research through academic support and tutoring. It "promotes effective partnerships between institutions to enhance the quality and quantity of underrepresented minority students who are being trained as the next generation of scientists."

http://www.nigms.nih.gov/minority/bridges.html

• **ENLACE Program.** Sponsored by the W. K. Kellogg Foundation, "ENLACE is a multiyear initiative designed to strengthen the educational pipeline and increase opportunities for Latinos to enter and complete college." The national program aims to serve as a catalyst to strengthen partnerships and create coalitions among HSIs.

http://www.wkkf.org/Programming/Overview.aspx?CID=16

• **Higher Education Opportunity Program (HEOP), N.Y.** HEOP provides services to New York State residents who, "because of academic and economic circumstances, would otherwise be unable to attend a postsecondary educational institution." HEOP serves those who are both academically and economically disadvantaged, and provides structured support services, including a prefreshman summer program; counseling; tutoring; remedial and developmental course work; and financial assistance for college expenses.

http://www.highered.nysed.gov/kiap/home.html

- **LifeMap, Valencia Community College, Orlando, Fla.** LifeMap is an individualized guide to help students determine when and how to take specific steps to complete degree requirements and attain career goals. LifeMap links all the components of the college—its faculty, staff, academic programs, technology, and services—in an effort to support students from admission through graduation and beyond.
  http://valenciacc.edu/lifemap/more_lifemap.asp

- **Mathematics, Engineering, Science Achievement (MESA).** The MESA USA partnership includes MESA programs from eight states that have joined together to support disadvantaged and underrepresented students to achieve academically in math, science, and engineering and to attain math-based degrees.
  http://mesa.ucop.edu

- **Program for Accelerated College Education (PACE), Calif.** Designed for the working student, PACE is a program offered at several colleges in the Los Angeles Community College District (LACCD). PACE assists students in earning an associate degree by providing a unique selection of academic courses presented in an accelerated format. PACE courses are offered one evening a week and on some Saturdays. All classes are university transferable and taught in eight-week sessions. The following links provide information about the PACE program at several LACCD campuses.
  http://www.glennvice.com/pace.htm
  http://www.piercecollege.edu/offices/Pace/Advisor.htm
  http://www.vcsun.org/~mpursley/pace

- **The Liberty Partnerships Program (LPP), N.Y.** Established in 1988, the LPP was a "legislative response to New York's school dropout rate." LPP goals include initiating partnerships between higher education institutions, public and private K–12 schools, parents, and other key stakeholders; improving the high school graduation rates of at-risk youth; and preparing disadvantaged students for competitive entry into higher education and the workforce.
  http://www.highered.nysed.gov/kiap/home.html

Recruitment and Retention Programs and Services

The following resources provide information and examples of effective minority student recruitment and retention programs and services.

- **Cañada College Student Retention Program, San Mateo, Calif.** Cañada has implemented a multistrand retention project that integrates curricular transformation, development and implementation of new teaching and learning strategies, online career assessment, and technological skills.
  http://www.canadacollege.edu

• **Gaining Early Awareness and Readiness for Undergraduate Programs (GEAR UP).** GEAR UP is a national competitive grant program through the U.S. Department of Education. Each year it awards grants to locally designed programs that create partnerships between colleges and middle schools serving low-income students in order to increase college attendance rates among low-income youth.

http://www.ed.gov/gearup

• **Go Centers, Tex.** Go Centers are a "grassroots network of community-managed college recruiting centers located in communities across the state of Texas." They operate as centers led by high school and college students with adult and higher education support, have physical facilities and computer connectivity linking them to online resources, and are organizational hubs for local marketing and outreach efforts. Go Centers also expand and develop partnerships between K–12 schools, higher education institutions, businesses, and other community organizations.

http://www.gocenter.info

• **Upward Bound.** A member of the federal TRIO program, Upward Bound is a precollege program that works with colleges to reach low-income and first-generation college students. It provides academic classes and college credit opportunities prior to college enrollment.

http://www.ed.gov/programs/trioupbound/index.html

Transfer Programs and Services

The following resources provide information about and examples of effective transfer programs and services for minority students.

• **Center for Community College Partnerships (CCCP), UCLA.** CCCP is responsible for developing and strengthening academic partnerships between UCLA and California community colleges, and seeks to coordinate a myriad of programs and services offered to community college transfer students. CCCP places specific emphasis on underserved populations and also develops and implements academic summer programs that help prepare minority students for transfer.

http://www.college.ucla.edu/up/cccp

• **Community College Academic Consortium, UCLA.** The Consortium, based out of UCLA's Center for Community College Partnerships, is "aimed at improving transfer rates for underrepresented, underserved, and low-income students" at several partner institutions in the Los Angeles area. The goals of the Consortium are to redesign curriculum and pedagogy in composition, mathematics, social science, and science through dialogue between community college and UCLA faculty.

http://www.college.ucla.edu/up/cccp/prog.htm

• **FACTS.org, Fla.** FACTS.org is "Florida's official online student advising system." High school and college students, parents, and academic and college counselors can use the services provided on this Web site to help plan progress through higher education in Florida. Launched in 2000, the online system was creating by the Florida Department of Education to "provide maximum access and seamless articulation services in order to help high school and college students make informed choices about their education." FACTS.org is provided free by the Florida Department of Education to help students make informed choices about their education.
http://www.facts.org

• **Puente Project, Calif.** Serving fifty-six community colleges and thirty-six high schools throughout California, Puente is a college preparatory program that provides services such as counseling, special academic classes, and mentoring. Puente emphasizes transfer to four-year colleges and a return to the community as a leader and mentor to future generations. The word *Puente* is Spanish for "bridge" and symbolizes the programmatic bridging between the community college and the university.
http://www.puente.net

• **Transfer Alliance Program (TAP), Los Angeles.** Based in Los Angeles, the Transfer Alliance Program is a collaborative program between UCLA and local community colleges that is designed for students who plan on transferring to UCLA. TAP provides special course sections designed for the academically interested and successful student. Services include a designated adviser and priority course registration.
http://www.admissions.ucla.edu/Prospect/Adm_tr/ADM_CCO/tap.htm

Financial Aid Programs and Services

The following programs and services assist minority students in paying for college.

• **California Work Opportunity and Responsibility to Kids (CalWorks).** The goal of CalWorks is to assist welfare recipients in gaining the education necessary to become self-sufficiently employed. The program sponsors skills classes in English, math, and ESL and offers GED preparation classes.
http://www.ccco.edu/divisions/ss/calworks/calworks.htm

• **Cooperative Agencies Resources for Education (CARE), Calif.** CARE assists single heads of household with children under fourteen years old who are recipients of California public assistance to attend and complete college. CARE supplies additional assistance in the form of allowances for child-care expenses, transportation, textbooks, and supplies.
http://www.ccco.edu/divisions/ss/care/care.htm

- **Extended Opportunities Programs and Services (EOP&S), Calif.** EOP&S is a California program that provides assistance to students who would likely never attend college without concerted help. Its purpose is to improve access and retention for low-income and educationally disadvantaged students. Benefits include additional counseling, priority registration, and assistance with all college costs.
   http://www.cccco.edu/divisions/ss/eops/eops.htm

- **Illinois Student Assistance Commissions (ISAC).** State lawmakers created ISAC to ensure that financial or educational barriers did not "prevent Illinois students from realizing their postsecondary educational goals." Since its inception in 1957, ISAC has gradually expanded its various programs and services, acting as a centralized source of information and guidance for students, families, and schools at all points in the education pipeline. Among such programs and services are state and federal grants, scholarships, and loans; college savings and investment options for families; and outreach and information services.
   http://www.collegezone.com.

- **Leveraging Educational Assistance Partnership (LEAP), Ariz.** Formerly the Arizona State Student Incentive Grant, LEAP is a "federal-state partnership to provide financial assistance in the form of grants to students who have demonstrated financial need." Each participating institution supplies matching funds equal to the amount of funds provided by the state for the LEAP program.
   http://www.azhighered.org/programs/ssig.html

References

Bradburn, E. M., and Hurst, D. G. *Community College Transfer Rates to Four-Year Institutions Using Alternative Definitions of Transfer.* (NCES 2001–197) Washington, D.C.: National Center for Education Statistics, U.S. Department of Education, 2001. (ED 454 301)

Bryant, A. N. "ERIC Review: Community College Students: Recent Findings and Trends." *Community College Review,* 2001, *29*(3), 77–94. (ED 457 898)

California Postsecondary Education Commission. *Student Transfer in California Postsecondary Education.* Commission Report 02–3. 2002. http://www.cpec.ca.gov/completereports/2002reports/02–03.pdf. Accessed June 2, 2004. (ED 464 672)

Cuseo, J. B. *The Transfer Transition: A Summary of Key Issues, Target Areas and Tactics for Reform.* Rancho Palos Verdes, Calif.: Marymount College, 1998. (ED 425 771)

Education Commission of the States. *StateNotes: Transfer and Articulation Policies.* 2001. http://www.ecs.org/clearinghouse/23/75/2375.htm. Accessed June 2, 2004. (ED 456 884)

Kezar, A., and Eckel, P. *The Effect of Institutional Culture on Change Strategies in Higher Education: Universal Principles or Culturally Responsive Concepts?* Washington, D.C.: U.S. Department of Education, Office of Education Research and Improvement, 2000. (ED 446 719)

Kozeracki, C. A. "Studying Transfer Students: Designs and Methodological Challenges." In F. S. Laanan (ed.), *Transfer Students: Trends and Issues*. New Directions for Community Colleges, no. 114. San Francisco: Jossey-Bass, 2001. (ED 456 889)

Laanan, F. S. (ed.). *Transfer Students: Trends and Issues*. New Directions for Community Colleges, no. 114. San Francisco: Jossey-Bass, 2001. (ED 456 889)

Rendón, L. I. "Fulfilling the Promise of Access and Opportunity: Collaborative Community Colleges for the Twenty-First Century." In American Association of Community Colleges (ed.), *New Expeditions: Charting the Second Century of Community Colleges. Issues Paper no. 3*. Annapolis Junction, Md.: Community College Press, 2000. (ED 440 670)

Rendón, L. I. "Foreword." In J. Castellanos and L. Jones (eds.), *The Majority in the Minority: Expanding the Representation of Latina/o Faculty, Administrators, and Students in Higher Education* (pp. viii–xii). Sterling, Va.: Stylus, 2003.

Schuetz, P. "Emerging Challenges for Community Colleges." *ERIC Digest*, 2002. (ED 477 829)

Szelenyi, K. "Minority Student Retention and Academic Achievement in Community Colleges." *ERIC Digest*, 2001. (ED 451 859)

Townsend, B. "Redefining the Community College Transfer Mission." *Community College Review*, 2001, 29(2), 29–42. (EJ 635 636)

U.S. Department of Education, National Center for Education Statistics. *Profiles of Undergraduates in U.S. Postsecondary Institutions: 1999–2000*. NCES 2002–168. Washington, D.C.: U.S. Department of Education, Office of Educational Research and Improvement, 2002. (ED 468 124)

U.S. Department of Education, Office of Civil Rights. *2003 U.S. Department of Education Accredited Postsecondary Minority Institutions*, 2003. http://www.ed.gov/about/offices/list/ocr/edlite-minorityinst-as-vi.html. Accessed May 27, 2004.

Wassmer, R., Moore, C., and Shulock, N. *A Quantitative Study of California Community College Transfer Rates: Policy Implications and a Future Research Agenda*. Sacramento: California State University, Institute for Higher Education Leadership and Policy, 2003.

VICTOR SÁENZ *is a doctoral student in the Graduate School of Education and Information Studies at the University of California, Los Angeles.*

INDEX

Back Issue/Subscription Order Form

Copy or detach and send to:
Jossey-Bass, A Wiley Imprint, 989 Market Street, San Francisco CA 94103-1741

Call or fax toll-free: Phone 888-378-2537 6:30AM – 3PM PST; Fax 888-481-2665

Back Issues: Please send me the following issues at $29 each
(Important: please include ISBN number with your order.)

_____

_____

_____

$ _____   Total for single issues

$ _____   SHIPPING CHARGES: SURFACE   Domestic Canadian
                                       First Item $5.00 $6.00
                                       Each Add'l Item $3.00 $1.50
                   For next-day and second-day delivery rates, call the number listed above.

Subscriptions   Please __ start __ renew my subscription to *New Directions for Community Colleges* for the year 2____at the following rate:

U.S.	__ Individual $80	__ Institutional $165
Canada	__ Individual $80	__ Institutional $165
All Others	__ Individual $104	__ Institutional $239
Online Subscription		__ Institutional $165

**For more information about online subscriptions visit
www.interscience.wiley.com**

$ _____   Total single issues and subscriptions (Add appropriate sales tax for your state for single issue orders. No sales tax for U.S. subscriptions. Canadian residents, add GST for subscriptions and single issues.)

__Payment enclosed (U.S. check or money order only)
__VISA __ MC __ AmEx __ # _____Exp. Date _____

Signature _____ Day Phone _____
__ Bill Me (U.S. institutional orders only. Purchase order required.)

Purchase order # _____
                 Federal Tax ID13559302   **GST 89102 8052**

Name _____

Address _____

_____

Phone _____ E-mail _____

For more information about Jossey-Bass, visit our Web site at www.josseybass.com

CC126   Developing and Implementing Assessment of Student Learning Outcomes
Andreea M. Serban, Jack Friedlander
Colleges are under increasing pressure to produce evidence of student
learning, but most assessment research focuses on four-year colleges. This
volume is designed for practitioners looking for models that community
colleges can apply to measuring student learning outcomes at the classroom,
course, program, and institutional levels to satisfy legislative and
accreditation requirements.
ISBN: 0-7879-7687-3

CC125   Legal Issues in the Community College
Robert C. Cloud
Community colleges must be prepared for lawsuits, federal statutes, court
rulings, union negotiations, and other legal issues that could affect
institutional stability and effectiveness. This volume provides leaders with
information about board relations, tenure and employment, student rights
and safety, disability law, risk management, copyright and technology
issues, and more.
ISBN: 0-7879-7482-X

CC124   Successful Approaches to Fundraising and Development
Mark David Milliron, Gerardo E. de los Santos, Boo Browning
This volume outlines how community colleges can tap into financial support
from the private sector, as four-year institutions have been doing. Chapter
authors discuss building community college foundations, cultivating
relationships with the local community, generating new sources of revenue,
fundraising from alumni, and the roles of boards, presidents, and trustees.
ISBN: 0-7879-7283-5

CC123   Help Wanted: Preparing Community College Leaders in a New Century
William E. Piland, David B. Wolf
This issue brings together various thoughtful perspectives on the nature of
leading community colleges over the foreseeable future. Authors offer
suggestions for specific programmatic actions that community colleges
themselves can take to provide the quantity, quality, specializations, and
diversity of leaders that are needed.
ISBN: 0-7879-7248-7

CC122   Classification Systems for Two-Year Colleges
Alexander C. McCormick, Rebecca D. Cox
This critically important volume advances the conversation among
researchers and practitioners about possible approaches to classifying two-
year colleges. After an introduction to the history, purpose, practice, and
pitfalls of classifying colleges and universities, five different classification
schemes are presented, followed by commentary by knowledgable
respondents representing potential users of a classification system:
community college associations, institutional leaders, and researchers. The

final chapter applies the five proposed schemes to a sample of colleges for purposes of illustration.
ISBN: 0-7879-7171-5   ·

CC121   **The Role of the Community College in Teacher Education**
Barbara K. Townsend, Jan M. Ignash
Illustrates the extent to which community colleges have become major players in teacher education, not only in the traditional way of providing the first two years of an undergraduate degree in teacher education but in more controversial ways such as offering associate and baccalaureate degrees in teacher education and providing alternative certification programs.
ISBN: 0-7879-6868-4

CC120   **Enhancing Community Colleges Through Professional Development**
Gordon E. Watts
Offers a much needed perspective on the expanding role of professional development in community colleges. Chapter authors provide descriptions of how their institutions have addressed issues through professional development, created institutional change, developed new delivery systems for professional development, reached beyond development just for faculty, and found new uses for traditional development activities.
ISBN: 0-7879-6330-5

CC119   **Developing Successful Partnerships with Business and the Community**
Mary S. Spangler
Demonstrates that there are many different approaches to community colleges' partnering with the private sector and that when partners are actively engaged in tailoring education, training, and learning to their students, everyone is the beneficiary.
ISBN: 0-7879-6321-9

CC118   **Community College Faculty: Characteristics, Practices, and Challenges**
Charles Outcalt
Offers multiple perspectives on the ways community college faculty fulfill their complex professional roles. With data from national surveys, this volume provides an overview of community college faculty, looks at their primary teaching responsibility, and examines particular groups of instructors, including part-timers, women, and people of color.
ISBN: 0-7879-6328-3

CC117   **Next Steps for the Community College**
Trudy H. Bers, Harriott D. Calhoun
Provides an overview of relevant literature and practice covering major community college topics: transfer rates, vocational education, remedial and developmental education, English as a second language education, assessment of student learning, student services, faculty and staff, and governance and policy. Includes a chapter discussing the categories, types, and purposes of literature about community colleges and the major publications germane to community college practitioners and scholars.
ISBN: 0-7879-6289-9

CC111 How Community Colleges Can Create Productive Collaborations with
Local Schools
James C. Palmer
Details ways that community colleges and high schools can work together to
help students navigate the difficult passage from secondary to higher
education. Provides detailed case studies of actual collaborations between
specific community colleges and high school districts, discuss legal problems
that can arise when high school students enroll in community colleges,
and more.
ISBN: 0-7879-5428-4

CC110 **Building Successful Relationships Between Community Colleges and the
Media**
Clifton Truman Daniel, Hanel Henriksen Hastings
Explores current relationships between two-year colleges and the media
across the country, reviewing the history of community colleges'
relationships with members of the press, examining the media's relationships
with community college practitioners, and offering practical strategies for
advancing an institution's visibility.
ISBN: 0-7879-5427-6

CC109 **Dimensions of Managing Academic Affairs in the Community College**
Douglas Robillard, Jr.
Offers advice on fulfilling the CAO's academic duties, and explores the
CAO's faculty and administrative roles, discussing how to balance the
sometimes conflicting roles of faculty mentor, advocate, and disciplinarian
and the importance of establishing a synergistic working relationship with
the president.
ISBN: 0-7879-5369-5

CC108 **Trends in Community College Curriculum**
Gwyer Schuyler
Presents a detailed picture of the national community college curriculum,
using survey data collected in 1998 by the Center for the Study of
Community Colleges. Chapters analyze approaches to general education,
vocational course offerings, the liberal arts, multicultural education, ESL,
honors programs, and distance learning.
ISBN: 0-7879-4849-7

**NEW DIRECTIONS FOR COMMUNITY COLLEGES
IS NOW AVAILABLE ONLINE AT WILEY INTERSCIENCE**

What is Wiley InterScience?

Wiley InterScience is the dynamic online content service from John Wiley &
Sons delivering the full text of over 300 leading scientific, technical, medical,
and professional journals, plus major reference works, the acclaimed *Current
Protocols* laboratory manuals, and even the full text of select Wiley print books
online.

What are some special features of Wiley InterScience?

Wiley InterScience Alerts is a service that delivers table of contents via e-mail
for any journal available on Wiley InterScience as soon as a new issue is
published online.
Early View is Wiley's exclusive service presenting individual articles online as
soon as they are ready, even before the release of the compiled print issue.
These articles are complete, peer-reviewed, and citable.
CrossRef is the innovative multi-publisher reference linking system enabling
readers to move seamlessly from a reference in a journal article to the cited
publication, typically located on a different server and published by a different
publisher.

How can I access Wiley InterScience?

Visit http://www.interscience.wiley.com

Guest Users can browse Wiley InterScience for unrestricted access to journal
Tables of Contents and Article Abstracts, or use the powerful search engine.
Registered Users are provided with a *Personal Home Page* to store and
manage customized alerts, searches, and links to favorite journals and articles.
Additionally, Registered Users can view free Online Sample Issues and preview
selected material from major reference works.
Licensed Customers are entitled to access full-text journal articles in PDF, with
select journals also offering full-text HTML.

How do I become an Authorized User?

Authorized Users are individuals authorized by a paying Customer to have
access to the journals in Wiley InterScience. For example, a university that
subscribes to Wiley journals is considered to be the Customer. Faculty, staff and
students authorized by the university to have access to those journals in Wiley
InterScience are Authorized Users. Users should contact their Library for information on which Wiley journals they have access to in Wiley InterScience.

ASK YOUR INSTITUTION ABOUT WILEY INTERSCIENCE TODAY!